The History Boys

Alan Bennett first appeared on the stage in 1960 as one of the authors and performers of the revue *Beyond the Fringe*. His stage plays include *Forty Years On*, *Getting On*, *Habeas Corpus*, *The Old Country*, *Enjoy* and *Kafka's Dick*, and he has written many television plays, notably *A Day Out*, *Sunset Across the Bay*, *A Woman of No Importance* and the series of monologues *Talking Heads*. An adaptation of his television play *An Englishman Abroad* was paired with *A Question of Attribution* in the double bill *Single Spies*, first produced at the National Theatre in 1988. This was followed in 1990 by his adaptation of *The Wind in the Willows* and in 1991 by *The Madness of George III*, both produced at the National Theatre. His stage version of *The Lady in the Van* was seen in the West End in 1999.

ALAN BENNETT

The History Boys

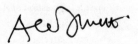

ff

faber and faber

First published in 2004
by Faber and Faber Limited
3 Queen Square London WC1N 3AU

Typeset by Country Setting, Kingsdown, Kent CT14 8ES
Printed in England by Mackays of Chatham plc, Chatham, Kent

A CIP record for this book
is available from the British Library

ISBN
0–571–22464–4 (pbk)
0–571–22472–5 (hbk)

4 6 8 10 9 7 5 3

Acknowledgements

My debt to Nicholas Hytner is, as always, profound: he encouraged me to finish the play and he put it into production well before he had a viable text. The cast, too, were both a joy and a help. I cannot remember rehearsals that I have enjoyed more since my last school play nearly forty years ago. It's a blessing that not many writers know what a good time you can have doing plays, or more people would be writing them.

I would also like to thank R. W. Johnson for permission to quote from his article in the *London Review of Books* and Professor George Steiner for letting me put some of his words into the mouth of Hector. I read *Lessons of the Masters* after I'd written the play and it was a great encouragement

Thank you, too, Neil Tennant and Chris Lowe, the Pet Shop Boys, who allowed Rudge in the play to do his version of one of their songs, 'It's a Sin' (I think their reputation is intact). There are many other quotations in the play, some of them buried and unattributed.

'Epitaphs of War, 1914–1918: Common Form', by Rudyard Kipling, is used by permission of A. P. Watt Ltd on behalf of The National Trust for Places of Historic Interest or Natural Beauty; 'Loveliest of Trees, the Cherry Now' and 'On Wenlock Edge the Wood's in Trouble', by A. E. Housman, by permission of The Society of Authors as the Literary Representative of the Estate of A. E. Housman; 'MCMXIV', by Philip Larkin, by permission of Faber and Faber Ltd; 'Mr Eliot's Sunday Morning Service', by T. S. Eliot, by permission of Faber and Faber Ltd; 'Musée des Beaux Arts' by W. H. Auden, by permission of Faber and Faber Ltd;

'Lullaby' by W. H. Auden, by permission of Faber and Faber Ltd; and 'Voices against England in the Night', by Stevie Smith, by permission of the Estate of James MacGibbon. Words and music for 'It's A Sin' by Neil Tennant and Chris Lowe © 1987 Cage Music Ltd, Sony/ATV Music Publishing (UK) Ltd. The extract from *Brief Encounter* is used by courtesy of Carlton International. We have been unable to trace UK copyright owners for permission to use the extracts from *Now Voyager* and *The Seventh Veil*, but will be happy to make these acknowledgements, and any others inadvertently overlooked, in future

Introduction

I have generally done well in examinations and not been intimidated by them. Back in 1948, when I took my O Levels – or School Certificate, as it was then called – I was made fun of by the other boys in my class because on the morning of the first paper I turned up in a suit. It was my only suit and already too small, but to wear it didn't seem silly to me then as I thought the examination was an occasion and that I must rise to it accordingly.

Ten years or so later I took my Finals at Oxford and dressed up again. This time, though, nobody laughed as we were all dressed up in the suit, white tie, mortar board and gown that were obligatory for the occasion. This was, I suppose, the last and most significant examination in my life, and it was in this examination that I cheated, just as I had cheated a few years before to get the scholarship that took me to Oxford in the first place.

I was not dishonest; I kept to the rules and didn't crib, and nobody else would have called it cheating, then or now, but it has always seemed so to me. False pretences, anyway.

I was educated at Leeds Modern School, a state school which in the forties and early fifties regularly sent boys on to Leeds University but seldom to Oxford or Cambridge. I don't recall the sixth form in my year being considered outstandingly clever but in 1951, for the first time, the headmaster, who had been at Cambridge himself, made an effort to push some of his university entrants towards the older universities. Snobbery was part of it, I imagine, and by the same token he switched the school from playing soccer to rugger, though since I avoided both this had little impact on me. However, there were about eight of us sixth formers who went up for the examinations and we all managed to get in, and some even to be awarded scholarships.

Though that's a situation which seems to mirror that of *The History Boys*, the play has nothing to do with my contemporaries, only a couple of whom were historians anyway, but it does draw on some of the pains and the excitement of working for a scholarship at a time when Oxford and Cambridge were as daunting and mysterious to me as to any of the boys in the play.

The first hurdle, more intimidating to me than any examination, was having to go up to Cambridge and stay in the college for the weekend. I had seldom been away from home and was not equipped for travel. I fancy a sponge bag had to be bought, but since at seventeen I still didn't shave, there wasn't much to go in it; my mother probably invested in some better pyjamas for me, but that was it. A stock vision of an undergraduate then (gleaned from movies like Robert Taylor in *A Yank at Oxford*) was of a young man in dressing gown and slippers, a towel round his neck, en route for the distant baths. I didn't run to a dressing gown and slippers either: 'Nobody'll mind if you just wear your raincoat,' my mother reassuringly said. I wasn't reassured but there was a limit to what my parents could afford.

It all seems absurd now, but not then. For all I knew someone who went to the baths in a raincoat and his ordinary shoes might not be the sort of undergraduate the college was looking for. And droll though these misgivings seem, then they were more real than any worries about the examination itself, and they persisted long after examinations were over, my social and class self-consciousness not entirely shed until long after my education proper was finished.

December 1951 was sunny but bitterly cold, and though there was no snow the Cam was frozen and the lawns and quadrangles white with frost; coming to it from the soot and grime of the West Riding, I had never seen or imagined a place of such beauty. And even today the only place that has enchanted me as much as Cambridge did then is Venice.

It was out of term, the university had gone down and apart from candidates like myself who had come up for the examination there was nobody about. But then that was true of most English country towns in the early 1950s, when tourism was not yet an option. I walked through King's, past Clare, Trinity Hall and Caius, and then through the back gate of Trinity and out into Trinity Great Court, and thought that this was how all cities should be. Nothing disconcerted this wondering boy, and I even managed to find the smell of old dinner that clung to the screens passage in the college halls somehow romantic and redolent of the past. And in those days one could just wander at will, go into any chapel or library, so that long after dusk I was still patrolling this enchanted place. Starved for antiquity, Hector says of himself in the play, and that was certainly true of me.

Gothick rather than Gothic Sidney Sussex, the college of my choice, wasn't quite my taste in buildings, but I was realistic about what I was entitled to expect both architecturally and academically, and (with Balliol the exception) the nastier a college looked the lower seemed to be its social and academic status. You had to be cleverer than I was or from higher up the social scale to have the real pick of the architecture.

It was unnerving to be interviewed by dons who had actually written books one had read. At Sidney it was the historian David Thomson with whose face I was familiar from the back of his Penguin. What surprised me, though, was the geniality of everyone and their kindness, though I'm familiar with it now, even as recently as this play. Being interviewed for Cambridge is not unlike being auditioned, only now my role is reversed. I hope I am just as genial and twinkling with our would-be performers as David Thomson and R. C. Smail were with me.

If the dons were genial, some of my fellow candidates were less so. That weekend was the first time I had ever come across public schoolboys in the mass, and I was appalled. They were loud, self-confident and all seemed to know one another, shouting down the table to prove it while also being shockingly greedy.

I had always found eating in public a nervous business, the way one was supposed to eat, like the way one was supposed to speak, a delicate area. I had only just learned, for instance, that the polite way when finishing your soup was to tip the plate away from you. I soon realised that this careful manoeuvre was not a refinement that was going to take me very far, not in this company anyway. Unabashed by the imposing surroundings in which they found themselves or (another first for me) being waited on by men, these boys hogged the bread, they slurped the soup and bolted whatever was put on their plates with medieval abandon. Public school they might be, but they were louts. Seated at long refectory tables, the walls hung with armorial escutcheons and the mellow portraits of Tudor and Stuart grandees, neat, timorous and genteel, we grammar school boys were the interlopers; these slobs, as they seemed to me, the party in possession.

Like Scripps in the play, on Sunday morning I went to communion in the college chapel, and in the same self-serving frame of mind, though in those days I would go to communion every Sunday anyway and sometimes midweek too. Asked in the interview what I was intending to do with my life, I think I probably said I planned to take Holy Orders. This was true, though I'm glad to say none of the dons thought to probe the nature of my faith, or they would have found it pretty shallow. And clichéd too, which Scripps' faith is not, besides being far more detached and sceptical than mine ever managed to be.

On the foggy way home I changed trains at Doncaster, where in a junk shop I bought my mother a little Rowlandson print of Dr Syntax pursued by bees. It was 7/6 and is probably not worth much more now, but it still hangs in the passage at home in Yorkshire, a reminder of that memorable weekend. A few days later I got a letter offering me a place at Sidney Sussex after I'd done my two years' National Service. It didn't work out like that, but at the time it all seemed very satisfactory. I was going to Cambridge.

At school I never had a teacher like Hector or like Irwin. My own history master was solid and dependable, his approach factual and down to earth, much as Mrs Lintott's. What drew me to him, though, was a hint of some secret sorrow. Mr Hill – H. H. Hill, the alliteration also a plus – was rumoured to have had some Housman-like breakdown at university when, having been expected to get a First, he had scarcely passed at all. That was as far as the Housman comparison would stretch, though, as he was happily married and fond of golf. An ironic and undemonstrative man, he was not temperamentally suited to the role of mentor or sage; still, he never made me feel a fool, which is high praise.

With other masters the secret sorrow was probably just that of middle-aged teachers in a not particularly good school with nothing to look forward to but retirement. Huddled at the bus stop waiting for the 4.15 to Horsforth, they looked a sad and shabby lot.

Once in a slack period of the afternoon when we were being particularly un-bright, the French master put his head down on the desk and wailed, 'Why am I wasting my life in this god-forsaken school?' It was not a question to which he expected an answer, and there was an embarrassed silence and a snigger from one of the less sensitive boys, much as there is in the play when Hector does the same. The incident stuck in my mind, I suppose, because it was a revelation to me at the time – I was fourteen or so –

that masters had inner lives (or lives at all). Teaching French, he looked French in a rather M. Hulot-like way, but was far from being an apostle of continental abandon. Not long before he had shepherded the class to a school showing of Marcel Carné's *Les Enfants du Paradis*, one of the earliest French films to be shown in Leeds after the war. Mystifying to me, it had deeply shocked him, and he had warned the class that those who led lives like the circus people in the film (fat chance) were likely to end up blind or riddled with disease. This just made me want to go back and see the film again, as I felt there must have been something that I'd missed.

That there were schoolmasters who were larger than life, whose pupils considered themselves set apart, only came home to me after I'd left school and was doing National Service. It was then, too, that I began to mix with boys who were much cleverer than I was and who had been better taught, all of us having ended up learning Russian at the Joint Services School. This, delightfully, was based at Cambridge, and while we officer cadets didn't quite lead the lives of undergraduates, service discipline was kept to a minimum in order to facilitate our Slavonic studies; we did not have to wear uniform or take part in parades, and in lots of ways it was a more easeful and idyllic existence than I was eventually to find university proper.

It was a heady atmosphere. Many of the others on the course were disconcertingly clever, particularly, I remember, a group of boys from Christ's Hospital – boys whose schools had been a world as mine never was; and when they talked of their schooldays there was often in the background a master whose teaching had been memorable and about whom they told anecdotes, and whose sayings they remembered: teachers, I remember thinking bitterly, who had presumably played a part in getting them the scholarships most of them had at Oxford and Cambridge. To me this just seemed unfair. I had never had such a teacher and had had to make my own way, which may be one of the reasons why I've been prompted to write such a teacher now.

As the months passed I began to feel that since I could hold my own with these boys in Russian maybe I ought to have another shot at getting a scholarship myself. Besides, I was at Cambridge already; perhaps, rather than come back there after National Service, I would be better (more rounded I fear I thought of it) going to Oxford. This first occurred to me in October 1953, and having written off for the prospectuses I found that I could take the scholarship examination at Exeter College, Oxford, in the following January.

There was no practical advantage to getting a scholarship. It carried more prestige, certainly, but no more money; at Oxford scholars wore a longer gown than commoners and had an extra year in college rather than in digs, but that apart I wanted a scholarship out of sheer vanity.

Or not quite. I had fallen for one of my colleagues with a passion as hopeless and unrequited as Posner's is for Dakin. This boy was going to Oxford on a scholarship, so naturally (or unnaturally as it was then) I wanted to do the same, and with some silly notion, again like Posner, that if I did manage to get a scholarship he would think more of me in consequence. Such illusions and the disillusions that inevitably came with them were, I see now, as significant as any examinations I did or did not take, and that underneath my formal education a more useful course of instruction was meanwhile in process.

If I was to take the examination at Exeter I didn't have much time. My history was rusty, and studying Russian during the day meant that the only time I had to myself was in the evenings, which I generally spent in the Cambridge Public Library. In the meantime I reduced everything I knew to a set of notes with answers to possible questions and odd, eye-catching quotations all written out on a series of forty or fifty correspondence cards, a handful of which I carried in my pocket wherever I went. I learned them in class while ostensibly doing Russian, on the bus coming into Cambridge in the mornings, and in any odd moment that presented itself.

When I went on Christmas leave just before the examination, I happened to find in Leeds Reference Library a complete set of *Horizon*, Cyril Connolly's wartime magazine which had ceased publication only a year or two before, but of which I had never heard. It opened my eyes to all sorts of cultural developments like existentialism which were then current and fashionable. I didn't understand them altogether, but these, too, got reduced to minced morsels on my cards in order to serve as fodder for the General Paper.

Come the examination, everything tumbled out: facts, quotations, all the stuff I'd laboriously committed to memory over the previous three months, my only problem being lack of time. At the interview I still said, as I had at Cambridge, that I would probably end up taking Holy Orders, though in view of the existentialism I spewed out it seemed increasingly unlikely.

When the letter came saying I'd won a scholarship I thought life was never going to be the same again, though it quite soon was, of course. The object of my affections was predictably unimpressed, and after my initial joy and surprise I began to feel the whole exercise had been a con on my part. I was a promising something, maybe, but certainly it wasn't a scholar.

Cut to three years later, when I'm two terms away from my final examinations in history. I hadn't had a notable university career either socially or academically, and I'd never had the same sense of life opening out as I'd had in the army. Now it was nearly over. I'd no idea what I wanted to do. Just as once I'd thought to become a vicar for no better reason than that I looked like one, so now it occurred to me I might become a don on the same principle. But to do that I had to perform much better in finals than I or my tutors expected me to do. Whatever had seemed unusual or promising about me when I'd been given a scholarship had long since worn off. I was a safe plodding second. I knew it and the college knew it too.

It was then that I remembered how I'd got the scholarship three years before, and as I began to cram for finals I adopted the same technique, reducing everything I knew to fit on cards which I carried everywhere, just as I'd done before. There were more cards this time but the contents were much the same: handy arguments, quotations, an examination kit in fact.

I also twigged what somebody ought to have taught me but never had, namely that there was a journalistic side to answering an examination question; that going for the wrong end of the stick was more attention-grabbing than a less unconventional approach, however balanced. Nobody had ever tutored me in examination techniques or conceded that such techniques existed, this omission I suspect to be put down to sheer snobbery or the notion (here ascribed to Hector) that all such considerations were practically indecent.

What we were supposed to be doing in the Final Schools was writing dry scholarly answers to academic questions. It's Mrs Lintott's method, with at Oxford a model answer often compared to a *Times* leader. In my case there wasn't much hope of that, with the alternative journalism of a lowlier sort, the question argued in brisk generalities flavoured with sufficient facts and quotations to engage the examiner's interest and disguise my basic ignorance. This is the Irwin method.

Once I'd got into the way of turning a question on its head in the way Irwin describes I began to get pleasure out of the technique itself, much as Dakin does, sketching out skeleton answers to all sorts of questions and using the same facts, for instance, to argue opposite points of view, all seasoned with a wide variety of references and quotations. I knew it wasn't scholarship, and in the Final Honours schools it would only take me so far, but it was my only hope.

I duly took the examination in scorching weather, two three-hour papers a day and the most gruelling five days of my life. At the finish I'd no idea how I had done and was so exhausted I didn't care and went to the cinema every afternoon for a week.

The results came out about six weeks later, after a *viva voce* examination. In those days everyone was viva'd, coming before the examining board even if it was only for half a minute, with a longer viva meaning that you were on the edge of a class and so likely to go up or down. Mine lasted half an hour and went, I thought, badly. I could see a couple of examiners were on my side and endeavouring to be kind; the others weren't interested. I went back home to Leeds in low spirits.

A friend who was in Oxford when the list went up sent me a postcard. It came on Monday morning when I was working at Tetley's Brewery, rolling barrels. My father was ill and out of work, and he and my mother brought this card to the lodge at the brewery gates, where I was sent for from the cellars. They weren't sure what a First was.

'Does it mean you've come top?' asked my mother, not particularly surprised, as from their point of view that's what I'd always done ever since elementary school.

I went back to pushing the barrels around, hardly able to believe my luck. It was one of the great days of my life, but it was luck. I was right: I hadn't done well in the *viva*, but another candidate had and with approximately the same results as mine had been put in the first class so I had to be included too. It was a narrow squeak.

With a First, a research grant was a formality, so I stayed on at Oxford and for a time even convinced myself I was a scholar, coming up twice a week to read manuscripts at the

Public Records Office, then still in Chancery Lane. But I was more a copyist than a scholar, since that was all I did, copying out medieval records with no notion what to do with them, and the longer I did it – for five years after taking my degree – the more dissatisfied with myself and the bigger fraud I felt. The truth was not in me.

However, in addition to my so-called research I did some college teaching, and though I wasn't much good at that either (and in today's more demanding conditions would soon have been stopped), I did at least try and teach my pupils the technique of answering essay questions and the strategy for passing examinations – techniques which I'd had to discover for myself and in the nick of time: journalism, in fact.

So *The History Boys* is in some sense an outcome of those two crucial examinations and the play both a confession and an expiation. I have no nostalgia for my Oxford days at all and am happy never to have to sit an examination again. In playwriting there are no examinations unless, that is, you count the *viva voce* the audience puts the actors through every night.

What sort of school is it that can send eight boys to sit for history scholarships at Oxford and Cambridge? Not a state school, surely, even in the 1980s? I wanted it to be, partly because that's how I'd imagined it, setting the action in my mind's eye as taking place in my own school, Leeds Modern School as was.

This last year while I was writing the play I used regularly to pass what had been the Modern School, now known as Lawnswood School. It was, almost symbolically I felt, in process of demolition, and the more I wrote of the play the less there was of the building. Now it has completely gone and been replaced by a new school built directly in front of the old site.

The process of demolition was protracted because, built in 1930, the building contained asbestos. This meant I couldn't pop in for one last look or to refresh my memory, until by chance *Look North* arranged to film me there a week or two before it was finally pulled down. I went along expecting it to seem smaller, which it duly did, but in memory it had a shine to it which had utterly vanished. Once there had been polished parquet floors the wood-work was of bright chestnut varnish, and particularly in the late afternoon (as was at one point mentioned in the play), the place took on a wonderful glow. Not now. It was shabby and dull and run-down.

The Headmaster, whom I had in my mind somehow blamed for the abandonment of the building, turned out to be helpful and understanding while not surprisingly being anxious to get out of what he saw as shabby and restrictive surroundings. I had no reason for nostalgia as the time I had spent in the school had been pretty dull and unmemorable, but still, it was a good building, and the facade should certainly have been incorporated in whatever re-placed it. Had it survived another ten or fifteen years it would certainly have been listed and preserved. Standing on the northern boundary of Leeds, it was always a hand-some and decent piece of thirties architecture, designed in the Municipal Architect's Department which in the thirties was one of the best in the country. I don't know who de-signed its replacement, but it has none of the old building's dignity and (this is the nub of it) none of its confidence. In 1930 the future of state education seemed assured. Now, who knows?

On the stage the school is vaguely taken to be in Sheffield, and in my head I called it Cutler's, and though there isn't a Cutler's Grammar School in Sheffield I feel there ought to have been. I made it a grammar school only because a comprehensive school would be unlikely to be fielding Oxbridge candidates in such numbers. Unlikely,

I subsequently found, to be fielding Oxbridge candidates at all, or at least not in the way I'd imagined.

When I was writing *The History Boys* I didn't pay much heed to when it was supposed to be set. While not timeless (though one always hopes), its period didn't seem important. It seemed to me to be about two sorts of teaching – or two teachers, anyway (characters always more important than themes), who were teaching more or less in the present; I could decide when precisely after I'd finished the play.

My own memories of sitting the Cambridge scholarship examination were so vivid that they coloured the writing of the play, with Oxford and Cambridge still held up to my sixth formers as citadels to be taken just as they were to me and my schoolfellows fifty years ago. I knew things had changed, of course, but I assumed that candidates for the scholarship examination spent two or three days at whichever university, staying in the college of their first choice, sitting a few examination papers and being interviewed: after which they would go back to Leeds or Blackburn or wherever to await the results ten days or so later. That was what had happened to me in December 1951, and it was a time I had never forgotten.

I was well on with the play when I mentioned it to a friend who had actually sat next to me in one of the scholarship examinations. He told me that I was hopelessly out of date, and that scholarship examinations such as we'd both experienced were a thing of the past, and even that scholarships themselves were not what they were. What had replaced the system he wasn't sure, but he thought that candidates no longer took scholarship examinations while they were at school, but at the end of their first year in college when awards were made on course work.

I was shocked and didn't want to know, not because this invalidated the play (it is a play, after all, and not a white paper), but because what had been such a memorable episode in my life was now wholly confined to history. What had happened so unforgettably to me couldn't happen any more; it was as outmoded as maypole dancing or the tram. And as for the now stay-at-home examinees, I just felt sorry for them. No romantic weekend for them, threading the frosted Backs or sliding over the cobbles of Trinity; no Evensong in King's: life as in so many other respects duller than once it was. I don't imagine the candidates themselves felt much deprived, and from the colleges' point of view it simply meant that they had another weekend available for conferences.

However, I now had to decide if I should adapt the play to present-day circumstances, but decided I shouldn't, as much for practical reasons as any concern for the facts. The current system of assessment, whatever its merits, is no help to the playwright. Graduated assessment is no use at all. The test, the examination, the ordeal, unfair though they may be, are at least dramatic.

Accordingly I set the play in the 1980s, when people seemed to think the system had changed. It's significant that without looking it up nobody I spoke to could quite remember the sequence, which testified to the truth of Irwin's remark about the remoteness of the recent past but is also an instance of how formless the history of institutions becomes once its public procedures are meddled with. Fairer, more decent and catering to the individual the new system may be, but memorable and even ceremonial, no, and that is a loss, though these days not an uncommon one.

Luckily the eighties were a period with no special sartorial stamp, no wince-making flares, for instance, or tie 'n' die. Mrs Thatcher was more of an obtruding presence then than she is in the play, but that particular omission will, I hope, be forgiven me.

The school is not a fee-paying grammar school such as Leeds or Manchester, which are both represented at the Headmasters' Conference and count as public schools. This, though, is what Mr Armstrong, the headmaster in the play, would aspire to, just as my own headteacher did all those years ago. I'm old fashioned enough to believe that private education should long since have been abolished and that Britain has paid too high a price in social inequality for its public schools. At the same time, I can't see that public schools could be abolished (even if there was the will) without an enormous amount of social disruption. The proper way forward would be for state education to reach such a standard that private schools would be undersubscribed, but there's fat chance of that, particularly under the present administration. The same hope, of course ought to animate the National Health Service, but the future for that seems equally bleak.

These days getting into Oxford or Cambridge or indeed any university is only the beginning of the story. Money has to be found, earned, donated by parents, borrowed from the bank or wherever student loans currently come from. It's a sizeable hurdle, and one my generation were happy to be without, if we ever gave it a thought. At that time acceptance by a university or any institution of higher learning automatically brought with it a grant from the state or the local authority. The names of the recipients of such grants would be printed in the local paper, occasionally with their photographs, the underlying assumption being that the names of these students should be known because they had done the state or the county some service and would now go on to do more. There was genuine pride in such achievements and in the free education that had made them possible – particularly perhaps in Leeds, which had an outstanding Education Department.

I am told that I am naive or unrealistic, but I do not understand why we cannot afford such a system today. As a nation we are poorer for the lack of it, the latest round in that lost fight the bullying through of the bill on top-up fees with this so-called Labour Government stamping on the grave of what it was once thought to stand for. Though there is much that is called education nowadays that is nothing of the sort and doesn't deserve subsidy, yet I still hold to the belief that a proper education should be free at the point of entry and the point of exit.

Some of these views can be put down to the circumstances of my own education but also to a book which made a great impression on me as a young man. This was Richard Hoggart's *The Uses of Literacy* (1955), and in particular his account of growing up in the slums of Leeds, going to Cockburn High School, and eventually to Leeds University, where be was taught by Bonamy Dobree. It was a harder childhood than mine (and an earlier one) but it was reading Hoggart forty years ago that made me feel that my life, dull though it was, might be made the stuff of literature. *The Uses of Literacy* spawned a series of books, one of which, *Education and the Working Class* by Jackson and Marsden, included a study of sixth form boys who had made it to university but not done well there, the conclusion being that the effort of getting to university often took so much out of working-class boys that once there they were exhausted. This is one of Posner's complaints in the play.

'The scholarship boy,' writes Hoggart, 'has been equipped for hurdle-jumping, so he merely thinks of getting on, but somehow not in the world's way . . . He has left his class, at least in spirit, by being in certain ways unusual, and he is still unusual in another class, too tense and overwound.' I had forgotten this passage until I found it quoted in *Injury Time*, one of the commonplace books of D. J. Enright, who must also have found it relevant to his own case.

Things have changed since Hoggart was writing, and the boys in the play are more privileged than Hoggart, Enright or me, but I suspect hurdle-jumping hasn't much changed, or the strain it engenders, though maybe it shows itself less in terms of class.

At Oxford in the late fifties some of the teaching I did was for Magdalen (which explains why it is occasionally mentioned in the text). One year I was also drafted in to help mark and interview candidates for the history scholarships. It didn't seem all that long since I had been interviewed myself, and I was nervous lest my marks should differ from those of my more experienced colleagues by whom I was every bit as intimidated as the candidates were.

I needn't have worried, though, as apart from the papers of authentic Wykehamist brilliance, the other promising candidates were virtually self-selecting, one's attention always caught by oddity, extremity and flair just as Irwin foresees. Whether these candidates were genuine originals or (like the boys in the play) coached into seeming so, the interview was meant to show up, but I'm not sure it always did. It was the triumph of Irwin.

Candidates do well in examinations for various reasons, some from genuine ability, obviously, but others because doing well in examinations is what they do well; they can put on a show. Maybe it doesn't work like that now that course work is taken into consideration and more weight is given to solider virtues. But it has always struck me that some of the flashier historians, particularly on television, are just grown-up versions of the wised-up schoolboys who generally got the scholarships (myself included). Here is R. W. Johnson, himself an historian, reviewing Niall Ferguson's *The Pity of War*:

> Both *The Pity of War* and the reception it has enjoyed illustrate aspects of British culture about which one can only feel ambivalent. Anyone who has been a victim, let alone a perpetrator, of the Oxbridge system will recognise Niall Ferguson's book for what it is: an extended and argumentative tutorial from a self-consciously clever, confrontational young don, determined to stand everything

on its head and argue with vehemence against what he sees as the conventional wisdom – or worse still, the fashion – of the time. The idea is to teach the young to think and argue, and the real past masters at it (Harry Weldon [Senior Tutor at Magdalen] was always held up as an example to me) were those who first argued under-graduates out of their received opinions, then turned around after a time and argued them out of their new-found radicalism, leaving them mystified as to what they believed and suspended in a free-floating state of cleverness.

R.W. Johnson, *London Review of Books*,
18 February 1999

I had friends at Magdalen who went through this dialectical de-briefing in their first year and it used to worry me that nothing remotely similar happened at Exeter. Nothing much happened at all until my third year, when in the nick of time I began to get grips with it myself. Still, I never thought of this as a proper education, just a way of getting through the examinations.

These considerations have acquired a more general interest as history has become more popular both on the page and on the screen. The doyen of TV historians, Simon Schama, is in a league of his own, and his political viewpoint is not in the forefront, but the new breed of historians – Niall Ferguson, Andrew Roberts and Norman Stone – all came to prominence under Mrs Thatcher and share some of her characteristics. Having found that taking the contrary view pays dividends, they seem to make this the tone of their customary discourse. A sneer is never far away and there's a persistently jeering note, perhaps bred by the habit of contention. David Starkey sneers too, but I feel this is more cosmetic.

None of this posing, though, is altogether new. A. J. P. Taylor was its original exponent, certainly on television, and was every bit as pleased with himself as the new breed of history boys. Still, with nothing else to put in the frame but his own personality and with no graphics and no film, he had perhaps more excuse for hamming it up a bit. His pleasure at his own technique, the flawless delivery (no autocue) and the winding-up of the lecture to the very second allotted were reasons enough for watching him, regardless of whatever history it was he was purveying. Even with him, though, the paradoxes and the contrariousness could get wearisome, certainly in the lecture hall, where I remember nodding off during one of his Ford Lectures.

Irwin's career path might seem odd. Schoolmaster to TV don is plausible enough, but from lecturing about the Dissolution of the Monasteries to Government spokesperson is a bit of a leap, though there are odder episodes in the early career of Alastair Campbell. No subject was further from my mind when I began to write the play, and it was only as I sat in on Irwin's classes, as it were, that I saw that teaching history or teaching the self-presentation involved with the examination of history was not unrelated to presentation in general.

The rehearsals for the plays were unusual in that the eight young actors playing the sixth-formers had to learn not only the parts they had to act but also what they meant. The play is stiff with literary and historical references, many of which, at first reading anyway, meant little to the actors. The early stages of rehearsal were therefore more like proper school than a stage version of it.

They read and talked about Auden, a favourite of Hector's in the play (though not of Mrs Lintott). Auden keeps being quoted, so we read and discussed some of his poems and the circumstances of his life. Hardy was another subject for tutorials, leading on to Larkin much as happens in the last scene of Act One. The First and Second Wars figure largely in the play, as they seemed to do on the classroom walls of the schools we visited to get some local colour before rehearsals started, so the period 1914–45 was also much discussed. I normally get impatient when there's a lot of talking before rehearsals proper start, but with this play it was essential.

Maybe, too, it says something about the status of the actor. Half a lifetime ago my first play, *Forty Years On*, though about a very different sort of school, was as full of buried quotations and historical allusion as *The History Boys*. Back in 1968, though, there was never any question of educating the score or so boys that made up Albion House School. We never, that I recall, filled them in on who Virginia Woolf was or put them in the picture about Lady Ottoline Morrell. Sapper, Buchan, Osbert Sitwell – to the boys these must have been names only, familiar to the principal players, John Gielgud and Paul Eddington, but as remote to the rest of the cast as historical figures in Shakespeare. This omission was partly because with only four weeks to rehearse there wasn't time to tell them more, but also because in those days actors were treated with less consideration than they are now, at any rate at the National Theatre.

But these early rehearsals with Nicholas Hytner taking the class were a reminder that good directors are often good teachers (Ronald Eyre is another example) and that theatre is often at its most absorbing when it's school.

Always beneath the play you write is the play you meant to write; changed but not abandoned and, with luck, not betrayed, but shadowing still the play that has come to be.

It is to Nicholas Hytner that I owe, among so much else, the idea for the original play, the one I didn't quite write, as it first came to me when I was listening to him being interviewed by Michael Berkeley on BBC Radio 3's *Private Passions*. Nick had earlier told me of his schooldays at Manchester Grammar School and how, having a good singing voice, he had sung in a boys' choir with the Hallé under Barbirolli. I was expecting him to talk about this on *Private Passions*, but rather to my disappointment he didn't. However, one of the records he chose was Ella Fitzgerald singing 'Bewitched' with its original Lorenz Hart lyrics, and it occurred to me at the time how theatrical this would sound sung by a boy with an unbroken voice.

This in turn took me back to my own childhood when, though I was no singer, I had been very slow to grow up, my own voice still unbroken when I was well past sixteen. So one of the history boys as first written was a boy much as I had been, a child in a class of young men. Nick (whose own voice broke at twelve) thought that these days a sixteen year-old boy with an unbroken voice was both unlikely and impossible to cast. This I could appreciate, though at the time I abandoned the notion with some regret.

The casting difficulty I can understand, but I don't entirely agree that such late development no longer occurs. It's true that today most children develop earlier, but the few who don't suffer more acutely in consequence, and it certainly still happens. I knew one boy, the son of a friend, who matured every bit as late as I did, though he coped with it much better than me. Looking back, I see those years from fourteen to sixteen as determining so much that I would later wish away, particularly a sense of being shut out that I have never entirely lost.

As it is, Posner is the heir to the character I never quite wrote, a boy who is young for his age and whose physical immaturity engenders a premature disillusion. Watching Sam Barnett playing the part, I wince to hear my own voice at sixteen.

A Note on the First Production

I have not included many stage directions or even noted
changes of scene; the more fluid the action the better.
The design of the National Theatre production, by Bob
Crowley, was of a classroom in a school built in the 1960s,
with the scenes in the staff room and Headmaster's study
achieved by re-arranging the sliding walls. These scene
changes were done largely by the boys themselves, under
cover of film sequences of life in the school projected on
a large video screen above the set proper. These, like the
opening shots of Irwin's TV series, *Heroes or Villains?*,
were filmed by Ben Taylor. Except for one moment
towards the end of Act Two, I have not given details of
these video inserts in the script, though they do often help
to move the action along: we see Dakin making up to
the Headmaster's secretary, for instance; Hector coming
disconsolately down the corridor after his dismissal; and
the start of his final trip on the motor bike.

There is a piano on stage throughout, and this, too, helps
to mask the scene change, besides accompanying the film
extracts which enliven Hector's eccentric teaching regime.

The History Boys was first performed in the Lyttelton auditorium of the National Theatre, London, on 18 May 2004. The cast was as follows:

Akthar Sacha Dhawan
Crowther Samuel Anderson
Dakin Dominic Cooper
Lockwood Andrew Knott
Posner Samuel Barnett
Rudge Russell Tovey
Scripps Jamie Parker
Timms James Corden

Headmaster Clive Merrison
Mrs Lintott Frances de la Tour
Hector Richard Griffiths
Irwin Stephen Campbell Moore

Other parts played by Tom Attwood, Rudi Dharmalingam, Colin Haigh, Joseph Raishbrook and Joan Walker

Director Nicholas Hytner
Designer Bob Crowley
Lighting Designer Mark Henderson
Music Richard Sisson
Sound Designer Colin Pink
Video Director Ben Taylor

The cover photograph includes members of the cast of this production. From back row to front: Russell Tovey, Andrew Knott, Jamie Parker, Samuel Anderson, Dominic Cooper, James Corden, Sacha Dhawan, Samuel Barnett

Characters

THE HISTORY BOYS

Act One

Irwin is in a wheelchair, in his forties, addressing three or four unidentified MPs.

Irwin This is the tricky one.

The effect of the bill will be to abolish trial by jury in at least half the cases that currently come before the courts and will to a significant extent abolish the presumption of innocence.

Our strategy should therefore be to insist that the bill does not diminish the liberty of the subject but amplifies it; that the true liberty of the subject consists in the freedom to walk the streets unmolested etc., etc., secure in the knowledge that if a crime is committed it will be promptly and sufficiently punished and that far from circumscribing the liberty of the subject this will enlarge it.

I would try not to be shrill or earnest. An amused tolerance always comes over best, particularly on television. Paradox works well and mists up the windows, which is handy. 'The loss of liberty is the price we pay for freedom' type thing.

School. That's all it is. In my case anyway. Back to school.

Though the general setting is a sixth-form classroom in a boys' school in the eighties in the north of England, when Hector first comes in, a figure in motor-cycle leathers and helmet, the stage is empty.

His sixth-formers, eight boys of seventeen or eighteen, come briskly on and take Hector out of his motor-cycle

3

gear, each boy removing an item and as he does so presenting it to the audience with a flourish.

Lockwood (*with gauntlets*) Les gants.

Akthar (*with a scarf*) L'écharpe.

Rudge Le blouson d'aviateur.

Finally the helmet is removed.

Timms Le casque.

The taking-off of the helmet reveals Hector (which is both his surname and his nickname) as a schoolmaster of fifty or so.
Dakin, a handsome boy, holds out a jacket.

Dakin Permettez-moi, monsieur.

Hector puts on the jacket.

Hector Bien fait, mes enfants. Bien fait.

Hector is a man of studied eccentricity. He wears a bow tie.

Classroom.

Now fades the thunder of the youth of England clearing summer's obligatory hurdles.

Felicitations to you all. Well done, Scripps! Bravo, Dakin! Crowther, congratulations. And Rudge, too. Remarkable. All, all deserve prizes. All, all have done that noble and necessary thing, you have satisfied the examiners of the Joint Matriculation Board, and now, proudly jingling your A Levels, those longed-for emblems of your conformity, you come before me once again to resume your education.

Rudge What were A Levels, then?

4

Hector Boys, boys, boys.

A Levels, Rudge are credentials, qualifications, the footings of your CV. Your Cheat's Visa. Time now for the bits in between. You will see from the timetable that our esteemed Headmaster has given these periods the euphemistic title –

Posner looks up the word in the dictionary.

– of General Studies.

Posner 'Euphemism . . . substitution of mild or vague or roundabout expression for a harsh or direct one.'

Hector A verbal fig-leaf. The mild or vague expression being General Studies. The harsh or direct one, Useless Knowledge. The otiose – (*Points at Posner.*) – the trash, the department of why bother?

Posner 'Otiose: serving no practical purpose, without function.'

Hector If, heaven forfend, I was ever entrusted with the timetable, I would call these lessons A Waste of Time.

Nothing that happens here has anything to do with getting on, but remember, open quotation marks, 'All knowledge is precious whether or not it serves the slightest human use,' close quotation marks.

Who said? Lockwood? Crowther? Timms? Akthar?

Pause.

'Loveliest of trees the cherry now.'

Akthar A. E. Housman, sir.

Hector 'A. E. Housman, sir.'

Timms Wasn't he a nancy, sir?

Hector Foul, festering grubby-minded little trollop. Do not use that word. (*He hits him on the head with an exercise book.*)

Timms You use it, sir.

Hector I do, sir, I know, but I am far gone in age and decrepitude.

Crowther You're not supposed to hit us, sir.
We could report you, sir.

Hector (*despair*) I know, I know. (*an elaborate pantomime, all this*)

Dakin You should treat us with more respect. We're scholarship candidates now.
We're all going in for Oxford and Cambridge.

There is a silence and Hector sits down at his table, seemingly stunned.

Hector 'Wash me in steep-down gulfs of liquid fire.'
I thought all that silliness was finished with.
I thought that after last year we were settling for the less lustrous institutions . . . Derby, Leicester, Nottingham. Even my own dear Sheffield. Scripps. You believe in God. Believe also in me: forget Oxford and Cambridge.
Why do you want to go there?

Lockwood Old, sir. Tried and tested.

Hector No, it's because other boys want to go there. It's the hot ticket, standing room only. So I'll thank you (*hitting him*) if nobody mentions Oxford (*hit*) or Cambridge (*hit*) in my lessons. There is a world elsewhere.

Dakin You're hitting us again, sir.

Hector Child, I am your teacher.
Whatever I do in this room is a token of my trust.
I am in your hands.
It is a pact. Bread eaten in secret.
'I have put before you life and death, blessing and cursing; therefore choose life, that both thou and thy seed may live.' Oxford and Cambridge!

6

He sits with his head on the desk, a parody of despair.

Posner (*Edgar*) 'Look up, My Lord.'

Timms (*Kent*)
'Vex not his ghost. O let him pass. He hates him
That would upon the rack of this tough world
Stretch him out longer.'

Posner (*Edgar*)
'O, he is gone indeed.'

Timms (*Kent*)
'The wonder is he hath endured so long.
He but usurped this life.'

Bell goes. Hector sits up.

Hector
'I have a journey, sir, shortly to go;
My master calls me, I must not say no.'

Posner (*Edgar*)
'The weight of this sad time we must obey
Speak what we feel, not what we ought to say.'

Timms The hitting never hurt. It was a joke. None of us cared. We lapped it up.

Crowther He goes mad.

Lockwood He hit me. He never hits me.

Rudge He hits you if he likes you. He never touches me.

Dakin (*happily*) I'm black and blue.

Scripps It's true what he said. I did believe in God.
Nobody else does. Like stamp collecting, it seems to have gone out and I suspect even the vicar thinks I am a freak.
But the big man is glad.
'The Prayer Book. *Hymns Ancient and Modern.* Lucky boy!'

7

Staff room.

Headmaster Mrs Lintott, Dorothy.

Mrs Lintott Headmaster?

Headmaster These Oxbridge boys. Your historians. Any special plans?

Mrs Lintott Their A Levels are very good.

Headmaster Their A Levels are *very* good. And that is thanks to you, Dorothy. We've never had so many. Remarkable! But what now – in teaching terms?

Mrs Lintott More of the same?

Headmaster Oh. Do you think so?

Mrs Lintott It's what we've done before.

Headmaster Quite. Without much success. No one last year. None the year before. When did we last have anyone in history at Oxford and Cambridge?

Mrs Lintott I tend not to distinguish.

Headmaster Between Oxford and Cambridge?

Mrs Lintott Between centres of higher learning. Last year two at Bristol, one at York. The year before . . .

Headmaster Yes, yes. I know that, Dorothy. But I am thinking league tables. Open scholarships. Reports to the Governors. I want them to do themselves justice. I want them to do you justice. Factually tip-top as your boys always are, something more is required.

Mrs Lintott More?

Headmaster Different.
    I would call it grooming did not that have overtones of the monkey house.
    'Presentation' might be the word.

8

Mrs Lintott They know their stuff. Plainly stated and properly organised facts need no presentation, surely.

Headmaster Oh, Dorothy. I think they do.
'The facts: serving suggestion.'

Mrs Lintott A sprig of parsley, you mean? Or an umbrella in the cocktail? Are dons so naive?

Headmaster Naive, Dorothy? Or human?
I am thinking of the boys. Clever, yes, remarkably so. Well taught, indubitably. But a little . . . *ordinaire*?
Think charm. Think polish. Think Renaissance Man.

Mrs Lintott Yes, Headmaster.

Headmaster Hector.

The Headmaster leaves as Hector comes in.

Hector Headmaster.

Mrs Lintott Didn't you try for Cambridge?

Hector Oxford.
I was brought up in the West Riding. I wanted somewhere new. That is to say old. So long as it was old I didn't mind where I went.

Mrs Lintott Durham was good in that respect.

Hector Sheffield wasn't.
Cloisters, ancient libraries . . . I was confusing learning with the smell of cold stone. If I had gone to Oxford I'd probably never have worked out the difference.

Mrs Lintott Durham was very good for history, it's where I had my first pizza. Other things, too, of course, but it's the pizza that stands out.
And fog, would you believe, one morning inside the cathedral. I loved it.
I wish some of them were trying to go there.

9

Hector No chance.

Mrs Lintott No. Our fearless leader has made up his mind.

And they are bright, brighter than last year's. But that's not enough apparently.

Hector It never was, even in my day.

Mrs Lintott Poor sods.

Scripps I'd been on playground duty, so I saw him on what must have been his first morning waiting outside the study. I thought he was a new boy, which of course he was, so I smiled.

Then Felix turned up.

Irwin is a young man, about twenty-five or so.

Headmaster You are?

Irwin Irwin.

Headmaster Irwin?

Irwin The supply teacher.

Headmaster Quite so.

He beckons Irwin cagily into the study.

Scripps Hector had said that if I wanted to write I should keep a notebook, and there must have been something furtive about Irwin's arrival because I wrote it down.

I called it clandestine, a word I'd just learnt and wasn't sure how to pronounce.

Headmaster The examinations are in December, which gives us three months at the outside . . . Well, you were at Cambridge, you know the form.

Irwin Oxford, Jesus.

Headmaster I thought of going, but this was the fifties. Change was in the air. A spirit of adventure.

Irwin So, where did you go?

Headmaster I was a geographer. I went to Hull.

Irwin Oh. Larkin.

Headmaster Everybody says that. 'Hull? Oh, Larkin.' I don't know about the poetry . . . as I say, I was a geographer . . . but as a librarian he was pitiless. The Himmler of the Accessions Desk. And now, we're told, women in droves.

Art. They get away with murder.

They are a likely lot, the boys. All keen. One oddity.

Rudge. Determined to try for Oxford and Christ Church of all places. No hope. Might get in at Loughborough in a bad year. Otherwise all bright. But they need polish. Edge. Your job. We are low in the league. I want to see us up there with Manchester Grammar School, Haberdashers' Aske's. Leighton Park. Or is that an open prison? No matter.

Pause.

There is a vacancy in history.

Irwin (*thoughtfully*) That's very true.

Headmaster In the school.

Irwin Ah.

Headmaster Get me scholarships, Irwin, pull us up the table, and it is yours. I am corseted by the curriculum, but I can find you three lessons a week.

Irwin Not enough.

Headmaster I agree. However, Mr Hector, our long-time English master, is General Studies. There is passion there.

Or, as I prefer to call it, commitment. But not curriculum-directed. Not curriculum-directed at all.

In the circumstances we may be able to filch an hour. (*going*) You are very young.

Grow a moustache.

I am thinking classroom control.

Classroom. Music. Posner sings some Piaf.

Hector Où voudriez-vous travailler cet après-midi?

Rudge Dans un garage.

Boys Non, non.

Scripps Pas encore. Ayez pitié de nous.

Hector Dakin. Où voudriez-vous travailler aujourd'hui?

Dakin Je voudrais travailler . . . dans une maison de passe.

Hector Oo-la-la.

Boys Qu'est ce que c'est?
Qu'est-ce qu'une maison de passe?

Posner A brothel.

Hector Très bien. Mais une maison de passe où tous les clients utilisent le subjonctif ou le conditionnel, oui?

He motions to Dakin, who goes off.
Dakin knocks on door.

Voilà. Déjà un client!
Qui est la femme de chambre?

Posner Moi. Je suis la femme de chambre.

Hector Comment appelez-vous?

Posner Je m'appelle Simone.

Dakin knocks again.

Akthar Simone, le monsieur ne peut pas attendre.

Posner opens the door and curtseys.

Posner Bonjour, monsieur.

Dakin Bonjour, chérie.

Posner Entrez, s'il vous plaît.
Voilà votre lit et voici votre prostituée.

Hector Oh. Ici on appelle un chat un chat.

Dakin Merci, madame.

Posner Mademoiselle.

Dakin Je veux m'étendre sur le lit.

Hector Je voudrais . . . I would like to stretch out on the bed in the conditional or the subjunctive.

Dakin makes to lie down.

Posner Mais les chaussures, monsieur, pas sur le lit.
Et vos pantalons, s'il vous plaît.

Dakin Excusez-moi, mademoiselle.

Posner Oh! Quelles belles jambes!

Dakin Watch it.

Posner Et maintenant . . . Claudine (*Timms*).

Dakin Oui, la prostituée, s'il vous plaît.

Scripps plays piano accompaniment, a version of 'La Vie en Rose'.

Crowther Monsieur, je pensais que vous voudriez des préliminaires?

Dakin Quels préliminaires?

Posner Claudine. Quels préliminaires sont sur le menu?

Timms (*Claudine*) A quel prix?

Dakin Dix francs.

Timms (*Claudine*) Dix francs? Pour dix francs je peux vous montrer ma prodigieuse poitrine.

Dakin Et maintenant, pourrais-je caresser la poitrine?

Timms (*Claudine*) Ça vous couterait quinze francs.
Pour vingt francs vous pouvez poser votre bouche sur ma poitrine en agitant . . .

Lockwood En agitant quoi?

There is a knock at the door.

Posner Un autre client. (*He lets them in.*)

Hector Ah, cher Monsieur le Directeur.

The Headmaster comes in with Irwin.

Headmaster Mr Hector, I hope I'm not . . .

Hector holds up an admonitory finger.

Hector L'Anglais, c'est interdit. Ici on ne parle que français, en accordant une importance particulière au subjonctif.

Headmaster Oh, ah.
Et qu'est ce-que ce passe ici?
Pourquoi cet garçon . . . Dakin, isn't it? . . . est sans ses . . . trousers?

Hector Quelqu'un? Ne soit pas timide. Dites à cher Monsieur le Directeur ce que nous faisons.

The boys are frozen.

Dakin Je suis un homme qui . . .

Hector Vous n'êtes pas un homme. Vous êtes un soldat . . . un soldat blessé; vous comprenez, cher Monsieur le Directeur . . . soldat blessé?

Headmaster Wounded soldier, of course, yes.

Hector Ici c'est un hôpital en Belgique.

Headmaster Belgique? Pourquoi Belgique?

Akthar À Ypres, sir. Ypres. Pendant la Guerre Mondiale Numéro *Une*.

Hector C'est ça. Dakin est un soldat blessé, un mutilé de guerre et les autres sont des médecins, infirmières et tout le personnel d'un grand établissement médical et thérapeutique.

Continuez, mes enfants.

Headmaster Mais . . .

A boy begins to moan.

Akthar Qu'il souffre!

Lockwood Ma mère! Ma mère!

Akthar Il appelle sa mère.

Lockwood Mon père!

Akthar Il appelle son père.

Lockwood Ma tante!

Headmaster Sa tante?

Timms La famille entière.

Hector Il est distrait. Il est distrait.

Irwin Il est commotionné, peut-être?

The classroom falls silent at this unexpected intrusion.

Hector Comment?

Irwin Commotionné. Shell-shocked.

There is a perceptible moment.

Hector C'est possible. Commotionné. Oui, c'est le mot juste.

Headmaster Permettez-moi d'introduire M. Irwin, notre nouveau professeur.

Hector Enchanté.

Headmaster Ce que je veux . . .

Hector Veuille . . . veu . . . ille . . .

Headmaster Vei-uille. Enough of this . . . silliness. Not silliness, no . . . but . . . Mr Hector, you are aware that these pupils are Oxbridge candidates.

Hector Are they? Are you sure? Nobody has told me.

Headmaster Mr Irwin will be coaching them, but it's a question of time. I have found him three lessons a week and I was wondering . . .

Hector No, Headmaster. (*He covers his ears.*)

Headmaster Purely on a temporary basis. It will be the last time, I promise.

Hector Last time was the last time also.

Headmaster I am thinking of the boys.

Hector I, too. Non. Absolument non. Non. Non. Non. C'est hors de question. Et puis, si vous voulez m'excuser, je dois continuer la leçon. ~À tout à l'heure.

Headmaster looks at Irwin.

Headmaster Fuck.

They go as the bell goes.

Rudge It's true, though, sir. We don't have much time.

Hector Now, who goes home?

There are no offers.

Surely I can give someone a lift?
Who's on pillion duty?
Dakin?

Dakin Not me, sir. Going into town.

Hector Crowther?

Crowther Off for a run, sir.

Hector Akthar?

Akthar Computer club, sir.

Posner I'll come, sir.

Hector No. No. Never mind.

Scripps (*resignedly*) I'll come, sir.

Hector Ah, Scripps.

Hector goes.

Scripps The things I do for Jesus. (*As he goes he gives Dakin the finger.*)

Posner I'd go.
I'm never asked.

Dakin You don't fit the bill.

Timms Me neither.

Dakin I tell you, be grateful.

Irwin (*distributing exercise books*) Dull.
   Dull.
   Abysmally dull.
   A triumph . . . the dullest of the lot.

Dakin I got all the points.

Irwin I didn't say it was wrong. I said it was dull.
   Its sheer competence was staggering.
   Interest nil.
   Oddity nil.
   Singularity nowhere.

Dakin Actually, sir, I know tradition requires it of the eccentric schoolmaster, but do you mind not throwing the books? They tend to fall apart.

Crowther It's the way we've been taught, sir.

Lockwood Mrs Lintott discourages the dramatic, sir.
   'This is history not histrionics.'

Timms You've got crap handwriting, sir.
   I read Irwin as 'I ruin'. Significant or what?

Irwin It's your eyesight that's bad and we know what that's caused by.

Timms Sir! Is that a coded reference to the mythical dangers of self-abuse?

Irwin Possibly. It might even be a joke.

Timms A joke, sir. Oh. Are jokes going to be a feature, sir? We need to know as it affects our mind-set.

Akthar You don't object to our using the expression, 'mind-set', do you, sir? Mr Hector doesn't care for it. He says if he catches any of us using it he'll kick our arses from bollocks to sundown, sir.

   Irwin regards them for a moment or two in silence.

18

Irwin At the time of the Reformation there were fourteen foreskins of Christ preserved, but it was thought that the church of St John Lateran in Rome had the authentic prepuce.

Dakin Don't think we're shocked by your mention of the word 'foreskin', sir.

Crowther No, sir. Some of us even have them.

Lockwood Not Posner, though, sir. Posner's like, you know, Jewish.
It's one of several things Posner doesn't have.

Posner mouths 'Fuck off.'

Lockwood That's not racist, though, sir.

Crowther Isn't it?

Lockwood It's race-related, but it's not racist.

Akthar Actually, I've not got one either. Moslems don't.

Another pause while Irwin regards the class.

Irwin Has anybody been to Rome?
No? Well, you will be competing against boys and girls who have. And they will have been to Rome and Venice, Florence and Perugia, and they will doubtless have done courses on what they have seen there. So they will know when they come to do an essay like this on the Church on the eve of the Reformation that some silly nonsense on the foreskins of Christ will come in handy so that their essays, unlike yours, will not be dull.
Think bored examiners.
Think sixty, think a hundred and sixty papers even more competent than the last so that the fourteen foreskins of Christ will come as a real ray of sunshine.
Come the fourteen foreskins of Christ and they'll think they've won the pools.

Irwin pauses as before.

You should hate them.

Crowther Who, sir?

Irwin Hate them because these boys and girls against whom you are to compete have been groomed like thoroughbreds for this one particular race. Put head to head with them and, on the evidence of these essays, you have none of you got a hope.

Crowther So why are we bothering?

Irwin I don't know.
I don't know at all.
You want it, I imagine. Or your parents want it. The Headmaster certainly wants it.
But I wouldn't waste the money. Judging by these, there is no point.
Go to Newcastle and be happy.

Long pause.

Of course, there is another way.

Crowther How?

Timms Cheat?

Irwin Possibly.

The bell rings and he is going out.

And Dakin.

Dakin Yes, sir?

Irwin Don't take the piss.
There isn't time. (*He goes.*)

Timms What a wanker.

Dakin They all have to do it, don't they?

Crowther Do what?

Dakin Show you they're still in the game. Foreskins and stuff. 'Ooh, sir! You devil!'

Scripps Have a heart. He's only five minutes older than we are.

Dakin What happened with Hector? On the bike?

Scripps As per. Except I managed to get my bag down.
I think he thought he'd got me going. In fact it was my *Tudor Economic Documents, Volume Two*.

They stop talking as Posner comes up.

Posner Because I was late growing up I am not included in this kind of conversation. I am not supposed to understand. Actually, they would be surprised how much I know about them and their bodies and everything else.

Scripps Dakin's navel, I remember, was small and hard like an unripe blackberry. Posner's navel was softer and more like that of the eponymous orange. Posner envied Dakin his navel and all the rest of him. That this envy might amount to love does not yet occur to Posner, as to date it has only caused him misery and dissatisfaction.

Posner goes and they resume the conversation.

Dakin I wish sometimes he'd just go for it.

Scripps Posner?

Dakin Hector.

Scripps He does go for it. That's the trouble.

Dakin In controlled conditions. Not on the fucking bike. I'm terrified.

Scripps Of the sex?

Dakin No. Of the next roundabout.
Rudge is having sex, apparently.

Rudge Only on Fridays. I need the weekend free for rugger. And golf.

Nobody thinks I have a hope in this exam.

Fuck 'em.

Dakin Currently I am seeing Fiona, the Headmaster's secretary, not that he knows. We haven't done it yet, but when we do I'm hoping one of the times might be on his study floor.

Scripps Shit!

Dakin It's like the Headmaster says: one should have targets.

Staff room.

Mrs Lintott The new man seems clever.

Hector He does. Depressingly so.

Mrs Lintott Men are, at history, of course.

Hector Why history particularly?

Mrs Lintott Story-telling so much of it, which is what men do naturally.

My ex, for instance. He told stories.

Hector Was he an historian?

Mrs Lintott Lintott? No. A chartered accountant.

Legged it to Dumfries.

Hector Dakin's a good-looking boy, though somehow sad.

Mrs Lintott You always think they're sad, Hector, every, every time. Actually I wouldn't have said he was sad. I would have said he was cunt-struck.

Hector Dorothy.

Mrs Lintott I'd have thought you'd have liked that. It's a compound adjective. You like compound adjectives.

Hector He's clever, though.

Mrs Lintott They're all clever. I saw to that.

Hector You give them an education. I give them the wherewithal to resist it. We are that entity beloved of our Headmaster, a 'team'.

Mrs Lintott You take a longer view than most. These days, teachers just remember the books they discovered and loved as students and shove them on the syllabus. Then they wonder why their pupils aren't as keen as they are. No discovery is why. *Catcher in the Rye* is a current example. Or have I got the whole thing wrong?

Hector Maybe Auden has it right.

Mrs Lintott That's a change.

Hector Dorothy.
     'Let each child that's in your care . . .'

Mrs Lintott I know, '. . . have as much neurosis as the child can bear.'
     And how many children had Auden, pray?

Classroom.

Irwin So we arrive eventually at the less-than-startling discovery that so far as the poets are concerned, the First World War gets the thumbs-down.
     We have the mountains of dead on both sides, right . . . 'hecatombs', as you all seem to have read somewhere . . .
     Anybody know what it means?

23

Posner 'Great public sacrifice of many victims, originally of oxen.'

Dakin Which, sir, since Wilfred Owen says men were dying like cattle, is the appropriate word.

Irwin True, but no need to look so smug about it.
   What else? Come on, tick them all off.

Crowther Trench warfare.

Lockwood Barrenness of the strategy.

Timms On both sides.

Akthar Stupidity of the generals.

Timms Donkeys, sir.

Dakin Haig particularly.

Posner Humiliation of Germany at Versailles. Re-drawing of national borders.

Crowther Ruhr and the Rhineland.

Akthar Mass unemployment. Inflation.

Timms Collapse of the Weimar Republic. Internal disorder. And . . . The Rise of Hitler!

Irwin So. Our overall conclusion is that the origins of the Second War lie in the unsatisfactory outcome of the First.

Timms (*doubtfully*) Yes. (*with more certainty*) Yes.

   Others nod.

Irwin First class. Bristol welcomes you with open arms. Manchester longs to have you. You can walk into Leeds. But I am a fellow of Magdalen College, Oxford, and I have just read seventy papers all saying the same thing and I am asleep . . .

Scripps But it's all true.

Irwin What has that got to do with it? What has that got to do with anything?

Let's go back to 1914 and I'll put you a different case. Try this for size.

Germany does not want war and if there is an arms race it is Britain who is leading it. Though there's no reason why we should want war. Nothing in it for us. Better stand back and let Germany and Russia fight it out while we take the imperial pickings.

These are facts.

Why do we not care to acknowledge them? The cattle, the body count. We still don't like to admit the war was even partly our fault because so many of our people died. A photograph on every mantelpiece. And all this mourning has veiled the truth. It's not so much lest we forget, as lest we remember. Because you should realise that so far as the Cenotaph and the Last Post and all that stuff is concerned, there's no better way of forgetting something than by commemorating it.

And Dakin.

Dakin Sir?

Irwin You were the one who was morally superior about Haig.

Dakin Passchendaele. The Somme. He was a butcher, sir.

Irwin Yes, but at least he delivered the goods. No, no, the real enemy to Haig's subsequent reputation was the Unknown Soldier. If Haig had had any sense he'd have had him disinterred and shot all over again for giving comfort to the enemy.

Lockwood So what about the poets, then?

Irwin What about them? If you read what they actually say as distinct from what they write, most of them seem to have enjoyed the war.

25

Siegfried Sassoon was a good officer. Saint Wilfred Owen couldn't wait to get back to his company. Both of them surprisingly bloodthirsty.

Poetry is good up to a point. Adds flavour.

Dakin It's the foreskins again, isn't it? Bit of garnish.

Irwin (*ignoring this*) But if you want to relate the politics to the war, forget Wilfred Owen and try Kipling:

Akthar Thanks a lot.

Irwin

'If any question why we died,
Tell them because our fathers lied.'

In other words . . .

Timms Oh no, sir. With respect, can I stop you? No, with a poem or any work of art we can never say 'in other words'. If it is a work of art there are no other words.

Lockwood Yes, sir. That's why it is a work of art in the first place.

You can't look at a Rembrandt and say 'in other words', can you, sir?

Irwin is puzzled where all this comes from but is distracted by Rudge.

Rudge So what's the verdict then, sir? What do I write down?

Irwin You can write down, Rudge, that 'I must not write down every word that teacher says.'

You can also write down that the First World War was a mistake. It was not a tragedy.

And as for the truth, Scripps, which you were worrying about: truth is no more at issue in an examination than thirst at a wine-tasting or fashion at a striptease.

Dakin Do you really believe that, sir, or are you just trying to make us think?

Scripps You can't explain away the poetry, sir.

Lockwood No, sir. Art wins in the end.

The bell goes.

Scripps What about this, sir?

'Those long uneven lines
Standing as patiently
As if they were stretched outside
The Oval or Villa Park,
The crowns of hats, the sun
On moustached archaic faces
Grinning as if it were all
An August Bank Holiday lark . . .'

The others take up the lines of Larkin's poem, maybe saying a couple of lines each through to the end, as they go – but matter of factly.

Lockwood
'Never such innocence,
Never before or since,
As changed itself to past
Without a word –

Akthar
'– the men
Leaving the gardens tidy,

Posner
'The thousands of marriages
Lasting a little while longer:

Timms
'Never such innocence again.'

Irwin How come you know all this by heart? (*Baffled, shouts.*) Not that it answers the question. (*He goes.*)

27

Scripps So much for our glorious dead.

Dakin I know. Still, apropos Passchendaele, can I bring you up to speed on Fiona?

Scripps No.

Dakin She's my Western Front. Last night, for instance, meeting only token resistance, I reconnoitred the ground . . . Are you interested in this?

Scripps No. Go on.

Dakin As far as . . . the actual place.

Scripps Shit.

Dakin I mean, not onto it and certainly not into it. But up to it. At which point the Hun, if I may so characterise the fair Fiona, suddenly dug in, no further deployments were sanctioned, and around 23.00 hours our forces withdrew.
    Like whereas I'd begun the evening thinking this might be the big push.

Scripps You do have a nice time.

Dakin And the beauty of it is, the metaphor really fits.
    I mean, just as moving up to the front-line troops presumably had to pass the sites of previous battles where every inch of territory has been hotly contested, so it is with me . . . like particularly her tits, which only fell after a prolonged campaign some three weeks ago and to which I now have immediate access and which were indeed the start line for last night's abortive thrust southwards.

Scripps I can't take any more. Enough.

Dakin Still, at least I'm doing better than Felix.

Posner Felix?

Scripps Why? He doesn't . . .

Dakin Tries to. Chases her round the desk hoping to cop a feel.

Scripps I don't want to think about it.

Dakin He's only human.

Posner Actually, when you think about it the metaphor isn't exact. Because what Fiona is presumably carrying out is a planned withdrawal. You're not forcing her. She's not being overwhelmed by superior forces.
   Does she like you?

Dakin Course she likes me.

Posner Then you're not disputing the territory. You're just negotiating over the pace of the occupation.

Scripps Just let us know when you get to Berlin.

Dakin I'm beginning to like him more.

Posner Who? Me?

Dakin Irwin. Though he hates me. (*Goes.*)

Posner Oh Scrippsy. I can't bear to listen, but I want to hear every word. What does that mean?

Posner sings a verse or two of 'Bewitched' as Scripps plays and the class filters back.

Hector Well done, Posner. Now poetry of a more traditional sort.

Timms groans.

Timms groans? What is this?

Timms Sir. I don't always understand poetry.

Hector You don't always understand it? Timms, I *never* understand it. But learn it now, know it now and you'll understand it whenever.

Timms I don't see how we can understand it. Most of the stuff poetry's about hasn't happened to us yet.

Hector But it will, Timms. It will. And then you will have the antidote ready! Grief. Happiness. Even when you're dying.
　　We're making your deathbeds here, boys.

Lockwood Fucking Ada.

Hector Poetry is the trailer! Forthcoming attractions!

There is a knock on the door. Hector motions them to silence.

'O villainy! Let the door be locked!
Treachery! Seek it out.'

The door is tried.

Hector (*whispers, or does he even bother to whisper?*)
Knocks at the door?
In literature.
The Trial, for instance, begins with a knock. Anybody?

Akthar The person from Porlock.

Hector Yes.

Posner *Don Giovanni*: the Commendatore.

Hector Excellent.

Scripps Behold I stand at the door and knock.
Revelation.

Timms looks.

Timms Gone, sir.

Hector Good.

Timms (*to the others*) Irwin.

Hector Very often the knock is elided – the knock, as it were, taken as knocked.
Did the knights knock at the door of Canterbury before they murdered Beckett?
And maybe the person from Porlock never actually knocked but just put his or her head in at the window?
Death knocks, I suppose.
Love.
And of course, opportunity.
(*looking at his watch*) Now. Some silly time.
Where's the kitty?

Posner gets a tin and gives it to Hector.

Timms/Lockwood Oh, sir, sir.
We've got one, sir.

Hector Fifty p each.

Timms It's a good one, sir.

Lockwood You won't get this one, sir.

Hector That remains to be seen.

Timms We have to smoke, sir.

Hector Very well.

Scripps accompanies this scene on the piano.

Timms Gerry, please help me.

Lockwood Shall we just have a cigarette on it?

Timms Yes.

Lockwood lights the cigarettes and gives one to Timms.

Lockwood May I sometimes come here?

Timms Whenever you like. It's your home, too.
There are people here who love you.

Lockwood And will you be happy, Charlotte?

Timms Oh Gerry. Don't let's ask for the moon.
We have the stars.

*Hector pretends puzzlement, looks in the tin to count
the kitty.*

Hector Could it be Paul Henreid and Bette Davis in *Now
Voyager*?

Timms Aw, sir.

Hector It's famous, you ignorant little tarts.

Lockwood We'd never heard of it, sir.

Hector Walt Whitman. *Leaves of Grass.*

'The untold want by life and land ne'er granted
Now Voyager, sail thou forth to seek and find.'

Fifty p. Pay up.

Lockwood Shit.

Hector When you say shit, Lockwood, I take it you're
referring to the well-established association between
money and excrement?

Lockwood Too right, sir.

Hector Good. Well, I will now tell you how much shit
there is in the pot, namely sixteen pounds.

They go, leaving Rudge working.

Mrs Lintott Ah, Rudge,

Rudge Miss.

Mrs Lintott How are you all getting on with Mr Irwin?

Rudge It's . . . interesting, miss, if you know what I mean. It makes me grateful for your lessons.

Mrs Lintott Really? That's nice to hear.

Rudge Firm foundations type thing. Point A. Point B. Point C. Mr Irwin is more . . . free-range?

Mrs Lintott I hadn't thought of you as a battery chicken, Rudge.

Rudge It's only a metaphor, miss.

Mrs Lintott I'm relieved to hear it.

Rudge You've force-fed us the facts; now we're in the process of running around acquiring flavour.

Mrs Lintott Is that what Mr Irwin says?

Rudge Oh no, miss. The metaphor's mine.

Mrs Lintott Well, you hang on to it.

Rudge Like I'm just going home now to watch some videos of the *Carry On* films. I don't understand why there are none in the school library.

Mrs Lintott Why should there be?

Rudge Mr Irwin said the *Carry Ons* would be good films to talk about.

Mrs Lintott Really? How peculiar. Does he like them, do you think?

Rudge Probably not, miss. You never know with him.

Mrs Lintott I'm now wondering if there's something there that I've missed.

Rudge Mr Irwin says that, 'While they have no intrinsic artistic merit – (*He is reading from his notes.*) – they achieve some of the permanence of art simply by persisting and acquire an incremental significance if only as social history.'

Mrs Lintott Jolly good.

Rudge 'If George Orwell had lived, nothing is more certain than that he would have written an essay on the *Carry On* films.'

Mrs Lintott I thought it was Mr Hector who was the Orwell fan.

Rudge He is. Mr Irwin says that if Orwell were alive today he'd be in the National Front.

Mrs Lintott Dear me. What fun you must all have.

Rudge It's cutting-edge, miss. It really is.

Timms Where do you live, sir?

Irwin Somewhere on the outskirts, why?

Timms 'Somewhere on the outskirts,' ooh. It's not a loft, is it, sir?

Akthar Do you exist on an unhealthy diet of takeaway food, sir, or do you whisk up gourmet meals for one?

Timms Or is it a lonely pizza, sir?

Irwin I manage.
No questions from you, Dakin?

Dakin What they want to know, sir, is, 'Do you have a life?'
Or are we it?
Are we your life?

34

Irwin Pretty dismal if you are. Because (*giving out books*) these are as dreary as ever.

If you want to learn about Stalin, study Henry VIII.

If you want to learn about Mrs Thatcher, study Henry VIII.

If you want to know about Hollywood, study Henry VIII.

The wrong end of the stick is the right one. A question has a front door and a back door. Go in the back, or better still, the side.

Flee the crowd. Follow Orwell. Be perverse.

And since I mention Orwell, take Stalin. Generally agreed to be a monster, and rightly. So dissent. Find something, anything, to say in his defence.

History nowadays is not a matter of conviction.

It's a performance. It's entertainment. And if it isn't, make it so.

Rudge I get it. It's an angle. You want us to find an angle.

Scripps When Irwin became well known as an historian it was for finding his way to the wrong end of seesaws, settling on some hitherto unquestioned historical assumption then proving the opposite. Notoriously he would one day demonstrate on television that those who had been genuinely caught napping by the attack on Pearl Harbour were the Japanese and that the real culprit was President Roosevelt.

Find a proposition, invert it, then look around for proofs. That was the technique and it was as formal in its way as the disciplines of the medieval schoolmen.

Irwin A question is about what you know, not about what you don't know. A question about Rembrandt, for instance, might prompt an answer about Francis Bacon.

Rudge What if you don't know about him either?

Irwin Turner then, or Ingres.

Rudge Is he an old master, sir?

Timms 'About suffering, they were never wrong,' sir,
'The Old Masters . . . how it takes place
While someone else is eating or opening a window . . . '

Irwin Have you done that with Mr Hector?

Timms Done what, sir?

Irwin The poem. You were quoting somebody. Auden.

Timms Was I, sir? Sometimes it just flows out. Brims over.

Irwin Why does he lock the door?

They turn to each other in mock surprise.

Akthar Lock the door? Does he lock the door?

Lockwood It's locked against the Forces of Progress, sir.

Crowther The spectre of Modernity.

Akthar It's locked against the future, sir.

Posner It's just that he doesn't like to be interrupted, sir.

Crowther Creep.

Akthar You have to lock the doors, sir. We are a nation of shoplifters, sir.

Lockwood It's excrement, sir. The tide of.

Timms And there's sexual intercourse, too, sir. They do it at bus stops, everyone young going down the long slide to happiness endlessly, sir.

Akthar Free as bloody birds, sir.

Crowther Disgusting.

36

Irwin Does he have a programme? Or is it just at random?

Boys Ask him, sir. We don't know, sir.

Akthar It's just the knowledge, sir.

Timms The pursuit of it for its own sake, sir.

Posner Not useful, sir. Not like your lessons.

Akthar Breaking bread with the dead, sir. That's what we do.

Irwin What it used to be called is 'wider reading'.

Lockwood Oh no, sir. It can be narrower reading. Mr Hector says if we know one book off by heart, it doesn't matter if it's really crap. The Prayer Book, sir. *The Mikado*, the *Pigeon Fancier's Gazette* . . . so long as it's words, sir. Words and worlds.

Crowther And the heart.

Lockwood Oh yes, sir. The heart.
'The heart has its reasons that reason knoweth not,' sir.

Crowther Pascal, sir.

Lockwood It's higher than your stuff, sir. Nobler.

Posner Only not useful, sir. Mr Hector's not as focused.

Timms No, not focused at all, sir. Blurred, sir, more.

Akthar You're much more focused, sir.

Crowther And we know what we're doing with you, sir. Half the time with him we don't know what we're doing at all. (*Mimes being mystified.*)

Timms We're poor little sheep that have lost our way, sir. Where are we?

Akthar You're very young, sir. This isn't your gap year, is it, sir?

Irwin I wish it was.

Lockwood Why, sir? Do you not like teaching us, sir?
We're not just a hiccup between the end of university and the beginning of life, like Auden, are we, sir?

Dakin Do you like Auden, sir?

Irwin Some.

Dakin Mr Hector does, sir. We know about Auden.
He was a schoolmaster for a bit, sir.

Irwin I believe he was, yes.

Dakin He was, sir. Do you think he was more like you or more like Mr Hector?

Irwin I've no idea. Why should he be like either of us?

Dakin I think he was more like Mr Hector, sir.
A bit of a shambles.
He snogged his pupils. Auden, sir. Not Mr Hector.

Irwin You know more about him than I do.

Dakin
'Lay your sleeping head, my love,
Human on my faithless arm.'

That was a pupil, sir. Shocking, isn't it?

Irwin So you could answer a question on Auden, then?

Boys How, sir?
No, sir.
That's in the exam, sir.

Timms Mr Hector's stuff's not meant for the exam, sir.
It's to make us more rounded human beings.

Irwin This examination will be about everything and anything you know and are.
If there's a question about Auden or whoever and you

38

know about it, you must answer it.

Akthar We couldn't do that, sir.
That would be a betrayal of trust.
Laying bare our souls, sir.

Lockwood Is nothing sacred, sir?
We're shocked.

Posner I would, sir.
And they would. They're taking the piss.

Lockwood
'England, you have been here too long
And the songs you sing now are the songs you sung
On an earlier day, now they are wrong.'

Irwin Who's that?

Lockwood Don't you know, sir?

Irwin No.

Lockwood Sir!
It's Stevie Smith, sir. Of 'Not Waving but Drowning'
fame.

Irwin Well, don't tell me that is useless knowledge.
You get an essay on post-imperial decline, losing an
empire and finding a role, all that stuff, that quote is the
perfect way to end it.

Akthar Couldn't do that, sir.
It's not education. It's culture.

Irwin How much more stuff like that have you got up
your sleeves?

The bell goes.

Lockwood All sorts, sir!
The train! The train!

Scripps plays a theme from Rachmaninov's Second Piano Concerto.

Posner (*Celia Johnson*) I really meant to do it.
I stood there right on the edge.
But I couldn't. I wasn't brave enough.
I would like to be able to say it was the thought of you and the children that prevented me but it wasn't.
I had no thoughts at all.
Only an overwhelming desire not to feel anything at all ever again.
Not to be unhappy any more.
I went back into the refreshment room.
That's when I nearly fainted.

Irwin What is all this?

Scripps (*Cyril Raymond*) Laura.

Posner (*Celia Johnson*) Yes, dear.

Scripps (*Cyril Raymond*) Whatever your dream was, it wasn't a very happy one was it?

Posner (*Celia Johnson*) No.

Scripps (*Cyril Raymond*) Is there anything I can do to help?

Posner (*Celia Johnson*) You always help, dear.

Scripps (*Cyril Raymond*) You've been a long way away.
Thank you for coming back to me.

She cries and he embraces her.

Irwin God knows why you've learned *Brief Encounter*.

Boys Oh very good, sir. Full marks, sir.

Irwin But I think you ought to know this lesson has been a complete waste of time.

Dakin Like Mr Hector's lessons then, sir. They're a waste of time, too.

Irwin Yes, you little smart-arse, but he's not trying to get you through an exam.

Staff room.

Mrs Lintott So have the boys given you a nickname?

Irwin Not that I'm aware of.

Mrs Lintott A nickname is an achievement . . . both in the sense of something won and also in its armorial sense of a badge, a blazon.
     Unsurprisingly, I am Tot or Totty. Some irony there, one feels.

Irwin Hector has no nickname.

Mrs Lintott Yes he has: Hector.

Irwin But he's called Hector.

Mrs Lintott And that's his nickname too. He isn't called Hector. His name's Douglas, though the only person I've ever heard address him as such is his somewhat unexpected wife.

Irwin Posner came to see me yesterday. He has a problem.

Mrs Lintott No nickname, but at least you get their problems. I seldom do.

Posner Sir, I think I may be homosexual.

Irwin Posner, I wanted to say, you are not yet in a position to be anything.

Mrs Lintott You're young, of course. I never had that advantage.

Posner I love Dakin.

Irwin Does Dakin know?

Posner Yes. He doesn't think it's surprising. Though Dakin likes girls basically.

Irwin I sympathised, though not so much as to suggest I might be in the same boat.

Mrs Lintott With Dakin?

Irwin With anybody.

Mrs Lintott That's sensible. One of the hardest things for boys to learn is that a teacher is human. One of the hardest things for a teacher to learn is not to try and tell them.

Posner Is it a phase, sir?

Irwin Do you think it's a phase?

Posner Some of the literature says it will pass.

Irwin I wanted to say that the literature may say that, but that literature doesn't.

Posner I'm not sure I want it to pass.
  But I want to get into Cambridge, sir. If I do, Dakin might love me.
  Or I might stop caring.
  Do you look at your life, sir?

Irwin I thought everyone did.

Posner I'm a Jew.
  I'm small.
  I'm homosexual.
  And I live in *Sheffield*.
  I'm fucked.

Mrs Lintott Did you let that go?

Irwin Fucked? Yes, I did, I'm afraid.

Mrs Lintott It's a test. A way of finding out if you've ceased to be a teacher and become a friend.
   He's a bright boy. You'll see. Next time he'll go further. What else did you talk about?

Irwin Nothing.
   No. Nothing.

Mrs Lintott goes.

Posner.

Posner Sir?

Irwin What goes on in Mr Hector's lessons?

Posner Nothing, sir.
   Anyway, you shouldn't ask me that, sir.

Irwin Quid pro quo.

Posner I have to go now, sir.

Irwin You learn poetry. Off your own bat?

Posner Sometimes.
   He makes you want to, sir.

Irwin How?

Posner It's a conspiracy, sir.

Irwin Who against?

Posner The world, sir. I hate this, sir. Can I go?

Irwin Is that why he locks the door?

Posner So that it's not part of the system, sir. Time out. Nobody's business. Useless knowledge.
   Can I go, sir?

Irwin Why didn't you ask Mr Hector about Dakin?

Pause.

Posner I wanted advice, sir.
Mr Hector would just have given me a quotation.
Housman, sir, probably.
Literature is medicine, wisdom, elastoplast.
Everything. It isn't, though, is it, sir?

Scripps Posner did not say it, but since he seldom took his eyes off Dakin, he knew that Irwin looked at him occasionally too and he wanted him to say so. Basically he just wanted company.

Irwin It will pass.

Posner Yes, sir.

Irwin And Posner.

Posner Sir?

Irwin You must try and acquire the habit of contradiction. You are too much in the acquiescent mode.

Posner Yes, sir.
No, sir.

Posner accompanied by Scripps sings the last verse of 'When I Survey the Wondrous Cross'.

Dakin So all this religion, what do you do?

Scripps Go to church. Pray.

Dakin Yes?

Scripps It's so time-consuming. You've no idea.

Dakin What else?

Scripps It's what you don't do.

Dakin You don't not wank?

Jesus. You're headed for the bin.

Scripps It's not for ever.

Dakin Yeah? Just tell me on the big day and I'll stand well back.

Scripps I figure I have to get through this romance with God now or else it'll be hanging around half my life. But I don't see why I should wish it on any other poor sod.

The parents, of course, hate it. So ageing.

Drugs they were prepared for, but not Matins.

Some of it, though, I still don't get. They reckon you have to love God because God loves you. Why? Posner loves you but it doesn't mean you have to love Posner. As it is, God's this massive case of unrequited love. He's Hector minus the motorbike.

God should get real. We don't owe him anything.

Dakin Good thing to say at Cambridge, that.

Scripps No.

Dakin Why? It's an angle.

Scripps It's private.

Dakin Fuck private.

Scripps Don't let Hector hear you say that. You're his best boy.

Test me.

Dakin What on?

Scripps T. S. Eliot.

'A painter of the Umbrian School
Designed upon a gesso ground
The nimbus of the Baptised God.
The wilderness is cracked and browned

45

'But through the water pale and thin
Still shine the unoffending feet
And there above the painter set
The Father and the Paraclete.'

Dakin This is the one about the painting in the National Gallery.

Scripps Yes.

Dakin Don't tell me.
Piero della Francesca.
Actually, you know what?
We are *fucking* clever.

Scripps (*laughs*) Do you know how to seem cleverer still?
Don't say Piero della Francesca. Just say Piero.

Dakin Yes?

Scripps Apparently.

Dakin Like Elvis.

Scripps You've got it.

Dakin The more you read, though, the more you see that literature is actually about losers.

Scripps No.

Dakin It's consolation. All literature is consolation.

Scripps No, it isn't. What about when it's celebration? Joy?

Dakin But it's written when the joy is over. Finished. So even when it's joy, it's grief. It's consolation.
That's why it gets written down.
I tell you, whatever Hector says, I find literature really lowering.

Scripps Do you really believe this?

46

Dakin Yes.

Scripps You're not just doing a line of stuff for the exam? Original thoughts?

Dakin No.

Scripps Because it's the kind of angle Irwin would come up with.

Dakin Well, it's true he was the one who made me realise you were allowed to think like this. He sanctioned it.
I didn't know you were allowed to call art and literature into question.

Scripps Think the unthinkable. Who's going to stop you? Only don't mention it to Hector.

Dakin *No*.

Scripps But if you reckon literature's consolation, you should try religion.

Dakin Actually it isn't wholly my idea.

Scripps No?

Dakin I've been reading this book by Kneeshaw.

Scripps Who?

Dakin (*shows him book*) Kneeshaw. He's a philosopher. Frederick Kneeshaw.

Scripps I think that's pronounced Nietszche.

Dakin Shit. Shit. Shit.

Scripps What's the matter?

Dakin I talked to Irwin about it. He didn't correct me. He let me call him Kneeshaw. He'll think I'm a right fool. Shit.

Irwin and Hector.

Irwin It's just that the boys seem to know more than they're telling.

Hector Don't most boys?
Diffidence is surely to be encouraged.

Irwin In an examination?
They seem to have got hold of the notion that the stuff they do with you is off-limits so far as the examination is concerned.

Hector That's hardly surprising. I count examinations, even for Oxford and Cambridge, as the enemy of education. Which is not to say that I don't regard education as the enemy of education, too.
However, if you think it will help, I will speak to them.

Irwin I'd appreciate it.
For what it's worth, I sympathise with your feelings about examinations, but they are a fact of life. I'm sure you want them to do well and the gobbets you have taught them might just tip the balance.

Hector What did you call them?
Gobbets? Is that what you think they are, gobbets?
Handy little quotes that can be trotted out to make a point?
Gobbets?
Codes, spells, runes – call them what you like, but do not call them *gobbets*.

Irwin I just thought it would be useful . . .

Hector Oh, it would be useful . . . every answer a Christmas tree hung with the appropriate gobbets. Except that they're learned *by heart*. And that is where they belong and like the other components of the heart not to be defiled by being trotted out to order.

Irwin So what are they meant to be storing them up for, these boys? Education isn't something for when they're old and grey and sitting by the fire. It's for now. The exam is next month.

Hector And what happens after the exam? Life goes on. Gobbets!

Headmaster and Irwin.

Headmaster How are our young men doing? Are they 'on stream'?

Irwin I think so.

Headmaster You think so? Are they or aren't they?

Irwin It must always be something of a lottery.

Headmaster A lottery? I don't like the sound of that, Irwin. I don't want you to fuck up. We have been down that road too many times before.

Irwin I'm not sure the boys are bringing as much from Mr Hector's classes as they might.

Headmaster You're lucky if they bring anything at all, but I don't know that it matters. Mr Hector has an old-fashioned faith in the redemptive power of words. In my experience, Oxbridge examiners are on the lookout for something altogether snappier.

After all, it's not how much literature that they know. What matters is how much they know *about* literature.

Chant the stuff till they're blue in the face, what good does it do?

Dorothy.

Mrs Lintott has appeared and the Headmaster goes.

Mrs Lintott One thing you will learn if you plan to stay in this benighted profession is that the chief enemy of culture in any school is always the Headmaster. Forgive Hector. He is trying to be the kind of teacher pupils will remember. Someone they will look back on. He impinges. Which is something one will never do.

Irwin But it's all about holding back. Not divulging. Something up their sleeve.

Mrs Lintott I wouldn't worry about that. Who's the best? Dakin?

Irwin He's the canniest.

Mrs Lintott And the best-looking.

Irwin Is he? I always have the impression he knows more than I do.

Mrs Lintott I'm sure he does.
   In every respect. He's currently seeing (if that is the word) the Headmaster's secretary.

Irwin I didn't know that.

Mrs Lintott Which means he probably knows a good deal more than any of us. Not surprising, really.

Irwin No.

Mrs Lintott One ought to know these things.

Irwin Yes.

Mrs Lintott Posner knows, I'm sure.

Scripps About halfway through that term something happened. Felix in a bate, Hector summoned, Fiona relegated to the outer office.

Hector I am summoned to the Presence. The Headmaster wishes to see me, whose library books, we must always remember, Larkin himself must on occasion have stamped. 'After such knowledge, what forgiveness?'

Headmaster You teach behind locked doors.

Hector On occasion.

Headmaster Why is that?

Hector I don't want to be interrupted.

Headmaster Teaching?

Pause.

Hector I beg your pardon?

Headmaster I am very angry.
   My wife, Mrs Armstrong, does voluntary work.
   One afternoon a week at the charity shop.
   Normally Mondays. Except this week she did Wednesday as well.
   The charity shop is not busy.
   She reads, naturally, but periodically she looks out of the window.
   Are you following me?
   The road. The traffic lights. And so on.

Pause.

On three occasions now she has seen a motorbike.
   Boy on pillion.
   A man . . . fiddling.
   Yesterday she took the number.
   For the moment I propose to say nothing about this, but fortunately it is not long before you are due to retire. In the circumstances I propose we bring that forward. I think we should be looking at the end of term.
   Have you nothing to say?

Hector

'The tree of man was never quiet.
Then 'twas the Roman; now 'tis I.'

Headmaster This is no time for poetry.

Hector I would have thought it was just the time.

Headmaster Did I say I was angry?

Hector I believe you did, yes.

Headmaster Did you not *think*?

Hector Ah, think.

'To think that two and two are four
And never five nor three
The heart of man has long been sore
And long 'tis like to be.'

Headmaster You are incorrigible.
I am assuming your wife doesn't know?

Hector I have no idea. What women know or don't
know has always been a mystery to me.
Incidentally, she helps out at the charity shop, too.
They all seem to do nowadays.
Philanthropy and its forms.

Headmaster And are you going to tell her?

Hector I don't know.
I'm not sure she'd be interested.

Headmaster Well, there's another thing.
Strange how even the most tragic turns of events
generally resolve themselves into questions about the
timetable. Irwin has been badgering me for more lessons.
In the circumstances a concession might be in order. In
the future, I think you and he might share.

Hector Share?

52

Headmaster Share.

Your teaching, however effective it may or may not have been, has always seemed to me to be selfish, less to do with the interests of the boys than some cockeyed notion you have about culture.

Sharing may correct that. In the meantime you must consider your position. I do not want to sack you. It's so untidy. It would be easier for all concerned if you retired early.

Hector is going.

Hector Nothing happened.

Headmaster A hand on a boy's genitals at fifty miles an hour, and you call it nothing?

Hector The transmission of knowledge is in itself an erotic act. In the Renaissance . . .

Headmaster Fuck the Renaissance. And fuck literature and Plato and Michaelangelo and Oscar Wilde and all the other shrunken violets you people line up. This is a school and it isn't normal.

Hector has just seen the Headmaster and, having got into his motorcycle gear, is sitting alone in the classroom.
Posner comes in.

Hector Ah, Posner.
No Dakin?

Posner With Mr Irwin, sir.

Hector Of course.

Posner They're going through old exam papers. Picking out questions.

53

Hector Ah.

Pornography.

No matter. We must carry on the fight without him. What have we learned this week?

Posner 'Drummer Hodge', sir.

Hardy.

Hector Oh. Nice.

Posner says the poem off by heart

'They throw in Drummer Hodge, to rest
Uncoffined – just as found:
His landmark is a kopje-crest
That breaks the veldt around;
And foreign constellations west
Each night above his mound.

'Young Hodge the Drummer never knew –
Fresh from his Wessex home –
The meaning of the broad Karoo,
The Bush, the dusty loam,
And why uprose to nightly view
Strange stars amid the gloam.

'Yet portion of that unknown plain
Will Hodge for ever be;
His homely Northern breast and brain
Grow to some Southern tree,
And strange-eyed constellations reign
His stars eternally.'

Hector Good. Very good. Any thoughts?

Posner sits next to him.

Posner I wondered, sir, if this 'Portion of that unknown plain / Will Hodge for ever be' is like Rupert Brooke, sir. 'There's some corner of a foreign field . . .' 'In that rich earth a richer dust concealed . . .'

54

Hector It is. It is. It's the same thought . . . though Hardy's is better, I think . . . more . . . more, well, down to earth. Quite literally, yes, down to earth.

Anything about his name?

Posner Hodge?

Hector Mmm – the important thing is that he *has* a name. Say Hardy is writing about the Zulu Wars or later the Boer War possibly, these were the first campaigns when soldiers . . . or common soldiers . . . were commemorated, the names of the dead recorded and inscribed on war memorials. Before this, soldiers . . . private soldiers anyway, were all unknown soldiers, and so far from being revered there was a firm in the nineteenth century, in Yorkshire of course, which swept up their bones from the battlefields of Europe in order to grind them into fertiliser.

So, thrown into a common grave though he may be, he is still Hodge the drummer. Lost boy though he is on the other side of the world, he still has a name.

Posner How old was he?

Hector If he's a drummer he would be a young soldier, younger than you probably.

Posner No. Hardy.

Hector Oh, how old was Hardy? When he wrote this, about sixty. My age, I suppose.

Saddish life, though not unappreciated.

'Uncoffined' is a typical Hardy usage.

A compound adjective, formed by putting 'un-' in front of the noun. Or verb, of course.

Un-kissed. Un-rejoicing. Un-confessed. Un-embraced.

It's a turn of phrase he has bequeathed to Larkin, who liked Hardy, apparently.

He does the same.

Un-spent. Un-fingermarked.

And with both of them it brings a sense of not sharing, of being out of it.

Whether because of diffidence or shyness, but a holding back. Not being in the swim. Can you see that?

Posner Yes, sir. I felt that a bit.

Hector The best moments in reading are when you come across something – a thought, a feeling, a way of looking at things – which you had thought special and particular to you. Now here it is, set down by someone else, a person you have never met, someone even who is long dead. And it is as if a hand has come out and taken yours.

He puts out his hand, and it seems for a moment as if Posner will take it, or even that Hector may put it on Posner's knee. But the moment passes.

Shall we just have the last verse again and I'll let you go.

Posner does the last verse again.
Dakin comes in.

And now, having thrown in Drummer Hodge, as found, here reporting for duty, helmet in hand, is young Lieutenant Dakin.

Dakin I'm sorry, sir.

Hector No, no. You were more gainfully employed, I'm sure.

Why the helmet?

Dakin My turn on the bike.
It's Wednesday, sir.

Hector Is it? So it is.
But no. Not today.
No. Today I go a different way.

'The words of Mercury are harsh after the songs of Apollo. You that way, we this way.'

Hector goes briskly off, leaving Dakin and Posner wondering.

Act Two

Irwin is about five years older and in a wheelchair; he is talking to camera.

Irwin If you want to learn about Stalin study Henry VIII.

If you want to learn about Mrs Thatcher study Henry VIII.

If you want to know about Hollywood study Henry VIII.

Music and video sequence.

This is Rievaulx Abbey and this vertiginous trench is its main latrine.

It is a sad fact that whatever the sublimity and splendour of the ruins of our great abbeys to the droves of often apathetic visitors the monastic life only comes alive when contemplating its toilet arrangements. (*He coughs and stops.*)

The Director comes on in outdoor gear, so that it's plain this is being filmed.

Director Are you okay?

Irwin Fine.

Director Sounding a tad schoolmasterly. Touch of the Mr Quelches. Smile-in-the-voice time, you know?

Irwin Yes?

Director Pick it up from 'the monastic life'.

Irwin The monastic life only comes alive when contemplating its toilet arrangements.

Not monks stumbling down the night stairs at three
in the morning to sing the first office of the day; not the
sound of prayer and praise unceasing sent heavenwards
from altar and cell; no, what fires the popular imagination
is stuff from the reredorter plopping twenty feet into the
drains.

God is dead. Shit lives.

Wanting toilet paper, or paper of any description, the
monks used to wipe their bottoms on scraps of fabric . . .
linen, muslin, patches of tapestry even, which presumably
they would rinse and rinse again before eventually
discarding them. Some of these rags survive, excavated
from the drains into which they were dropped five hundred
years ago and more, and here now find themselves
exhibited in the abbey museum.

The patron saint here, whose bones were buried at
Rievaulx, was Aelred. And it is conceivable that one of
these ancient arsewipes was actually used by the saint.
Which at that time would have made it a relic, something
at which credulous pilgrims would come to gaze.

But what are these modern-day pilgrims gazing at but
these same ancient rags, hallowed not by saintly usage,
it's true, but by time . . . and time alone? They are old
and they have survived. And there is an increment even
in excrement, so sanitised by the years and sanctified,
too, they have become relics in their own right . . . and
more pilgrims come now to see them and these other
remains than ever came in the age of faith.

We are differently credulous and our cults are not the
same but saner, wiser, more rational . . .

(*He stumbles again.*) I think not.

Sorry.

Director Not like you.

You're sure you're okay?

Irwin Fine.

Director Let's take five.

Irwin wheels himself back to someone who has been watching.

Irwin Familiar?

Man Some of it.

Irwin Meretricious, of course, but that's nothing new.

Man I've forgotten what meretricious means.

Irwin Eye-catching, showy; false.

Man But you were a good teacher.

Irwin The meretricious often are . . . on television particularly.
The wheelchair helps, of course.
Disability brings with it an assumption of sincerity.

Pause.

I hope they're paying you well.
Whose idea was it?

Man I have a counsellor. She thought it would help.

Irwin What happened at Oxford?

Man Cambridge.
It didn't work out.

Irwin I think I heard that.

Man All the effort went into getting there and then I had nothing left. I thought I'd got somewhere, then I found I had to go on.

Pause.

About the money, my counsellor said that if I was paid for it, that would be therapeutic.

Irwin I'm surprised anyone's interested.
It's not much of a story.

Man You're a celebrity. It doesn't have to be.

Irwin And did you write it yourself?

Man Yes. Well, I talked to someone from the paper.
You come out of it very well.

Irwin And Hector?

The Man says nothing.

Man I didn't say anything about you and Dakin.

Irwin Nothing happened between me and Dakin.

Man I think it did.

Irwin No. It's not true.

Man You used to say that wasn't important.

Pause.

You liked him.

Irwin says nothing.

I wondered if you wanted to talk about it.

Irwin Why? Nothing happened.

Man He liked you . . . didn't he?
Tell me, sir. I need to know.

Irwin Why? Why?

Pause.

Are you miked?

Man says nothing.

You're miked, aren't you?
Jesus.
How did you come to this?

Man They won't print it unless you say something.

Irwin Good.

Man It's a chance to tell your side of the story.

Irwin There is no story.

Man You don't want to seem like Hector.

Irwin I wasn't like Hector.
Now fuck off.
I must return to the world of Henry VIII. It suddenly seems almost cosy.

He is wheeling himself away.

Director Ready?

Man Sir.
Would you sign your book?

He has a book written by Irwin open.
Irwin shakes his head but takes the book.

Irwin Whom shall I put it to?

Man Me. David.

Irwin I never called you David. I called you Posner.
I'll put 'To Posner', if that doesn't seem unfriendly.
Which it is.

Posner (*appealing*) Sir.

The make-up assistant hustles Posner away. Irwin shakes his head again and goes back into the light.

Irwin Okay.

Director I'll cue you.

Irwin's Voice We are differently credulous and our cults are not the same . . . but saner, wiser, more rational . . . I think not.

Irwin Ours is an easier faith. Where they reverenced sanctity we reverence celebrity; they venerated strenuous piety; we venerate supine antiquity. In our catechism old is good, older is better, ancient is best with a bonus on archaeology because it's the closest history comes to shopping.

Whatever we tell ourselves, things matter to us more than people. Not the scattering of communities or the torments of the martyrs or the putting of an end to prayer, no, what shocks us today about the Dissolution is the loss of *things*. Which, since monasticism originated in a flight from things, is something of an irony. So that you could say that it was at the moment of the Dissolution that the monasteries came closest to the ideals of their foundation and that it was thanks to the villain Henry VIII that the monasteries achieved their purpose and their apotheosis.

A silence.

Director Lovely. Though we're still not sure about apotheosis.

Irwin It is BBC2.

Classroom.

Hector is in sombre and distracted mood.

Posner (*young*) 'Apotheosis: a perfect example of its type. Moment of highest fulfilment.'

Hector is miles away.

Sir. Apotheosis. Moment of highest fulfilment.

Hector Oh yes. Very good, dictionary person.

Now. Can I have your attention. I . . . I have something I have to . . . tell you.

Pause.

Akthar We know, sir.

Hector Oh.

Dakin About sharing lessons with Mr Irwin, sir?

Hector Ah.

Lockwood Why is that, sir?

Hector That?
Oh. It's just a question of timetable, apparently.
No. What I was going to tell you . . .

Lockwood What's the point, sir?
Your lessons are so different from his.
The whole ethos is different, sir.

Timms And we relish the contrast, sir.

Crowther Revel in it, sir.

Lockwood Yin and yang, sir.

Akthar The rapier cut and thrust, sir.

Timms It's all about variety, sir.

Hector Hush, boys. Hush. Sometimes . . . sometimes you defeat me.

Dakin Oh no, sir. If we wanted to defeat you we would be like Cordelia and say nothing.

Hector Can't you see I'm not in the mood?

Dakin What mood is that, sir? The subjunctive? The mood of possibility? The mood of might-have-been?

Hector Get on with some work. Read.

Lockwood Read, sir? Oh come on, sir. That's no fun.

Akthar Boring.

Hector Am I fun? Is that what I am?

Timms Not today, sir. No fun at all.

Hector Is that what you think these lessons are? Fun?

Lockwood But fun is good, sir.
You always say . . .

Posner Not just fun, sir.

Akthar (*pointing at Posner*) Would you like him to sing to you, sir? Would that help?

Hector Shut up! Just shut up. All of you.
SHUT UP, you mindless fools.
What made me piss my life away in this god-forsaken place? There's nothing of me left. Go away. Class dismissed. Go.

He puts his head down on the desk.
There are some giggles and face-pullings before they realise it's serious.
Now they're nonplussed and embarrassed.
Scripps indicates to Dakin that Hector is crying.
Scripps is nearest to him and ought to touch him, but doesn't, nor does Dakin.
Posner is the one who comes and after some hesitation pats Hector rather awkwardly on the back, saying, 'Sir.'
Then he starts, still very awkwardly, to rub his back.

Scripps I was the nearest. I ought to have been the one to reach out and touch him. But I just watched.
Dakin did nothing either. Neither of us did.

He looks at Dakin, who looks away.

Later I wrote it all down.

Hector sits up and blows his nose loudly.

Hector I don't know what all that was about, I'm sure.
Nothing is here for tears, nothing to wail.
I am an old man in a dry season. Enough.

The boys are still a bit abashed.

Timms These two have got something to cheer you up,
sir.

Dakin Oh yes. A film, sir.

Hector Oh, a film. Goody goody. And twenty-three
pounds in the kitty!

Dakin (*indicating Scripps*) He's the woman, sir.

Hector Off you go.

*Francesca (Scripps) is playing Beethoven's 'Pathétique'
Sonata on the piano. James Mason (Dakin), her
guardian, limps to the piano.*

Dakin Francesca. You belong to me. We must always be
together. You know that, don't you? Promise you'll stay
with me always. Promise.

She slowly shakes her head.

Very well. If that's the way you want it. If you won't play
for me, you shan't play for anybody ever again.

*He brings his stick down across her fingers on the
keyboard. She shrieks and rushes sobbing from the
room.*

Hector If I say Greig's Piano Concerto?

Dakin/Scripps No, sir.

Hector If I say *Svengali*?

Dakin/Scripps (*beginning to congratulate themselves*)
No, sir. No.

Hector And if I say 1945, James Mason and Anne Todd in *The Seventh Veil*?

Dakin/Scripps Aww, sir!

The other boys are delighted at their failure.

Hector Pay up, pay up and play the game!

The bell goes. Hector is left, after they've all cleared, sitting at the table.

Headmaster Did he say why he was going?

Mrs Lintott More or less.

Headmaster I am surprised. I have said nothing to anyone.
As I left it he was considering his position.
I hope he will go.

Mrs Lintott He would like to stay. To work out his time. That's what I wanted to ask.

Headmaster Shall I tell you what is wrong with Hector as a teacher?
It isn't that he doesn't produce results. He does. But they are unpredictable and unquantifiable and in the current educational climate that is no use. He may well be doing his job, but there is no method that I know of that enables me to assess the job that he is doing.
There is inspiration, certainly, but how do I quantify that? And he has no notion of boundaries. A few weeks ago I caught him teaching French. French!
English is his subject. And I happened to hear one child singing yesterday morning, and on enquiry I find his pupils know all the words of 'When I'm Cleaning Windows'. George Formby. And Gracie Fields. Dorothy, what has Gracie Fields got to do with anything?

So the upshot is I am glad he handled his pupils' balls because that at least I can categorise.

It is a reason for him going no one can dispute.

And I was so pleased on the night Mrs Armstrong told me she was startled to find she was the object of unaccustomed sexual interference herself. That is a measure of how pleased I was, though I shan't say that to the inspectors.

Mrs Lintott says nothing.

You didn't know. He hadn't told you why he was going?

Mrs Lintott Not that, no.

Headmaster I assumed you knew.

Mrs Lintott No.

Headmaster In which case you must keep it to yourself, both his going and the reason for it.

Mrs Lintott He handled the boys' balls?

Headmaster I don't want to spell it out. You've been married yourself, you know the form. And while on the motorbike. He, as it were, cradled them. To be fair it was I think more appreciative than investigatory but it is inexcusable nevertheless. Think of the gulf of years. And the speed! One knows that road well.

No, no. It's to everyone's benefit that he should go as soon as possible. (*He goes.*)

Mrs Lintott I have not hitherto been allotted an inner voice, my role a patient and not unamused sufferance of the predilections and preoccupations of men. They kick their particular stone along the street and I watch.

I am, it is true, confided in by all parties, my gender some sort of safeguard against the onward transmission of information . . . though that I should be assumed to be so discreet is in itself condescending. I'm what men would call a safe pair of hands.

Irwin comes in.

Our Headmaster is a twat. An impermissible word nowadays but the only one suited to my purpose. A twat. And to go further down the same proscribed path, a condescending cunt.

Do you think Hector is a good teacher?

Irwin Yes, I suppose . . . but what do I know?

Mrs Lintott You see, I probably don't. When I was teaching in London in the seventies there was a consoling myth that not very bright children could always become artists. Droves of the half-educated left school with the notion that art or some form of self-realisation was a viable option. It's by the same well-meaning token that it's assumed still that every third person in prison is a potential Van Gogh. And love him though I do I feel there's a touch of that to Hector . . . or what's all this learning by heart for, except as some sort of insurance against the boys' ultimate failure?

Not that it matters now, one way or another.

Irwin Why? What's happened?

Mrs Lintott Nothing. Nothing. (*She is going.*) Isn't this his lesson?

Irwin It is. But we're sharing, hadn't you heard?

Mrs Lintott Sharing? Whose cockeyed idea was that? Don't tell me.
Twat, twat, twat.

Boys come in, followed by Hector. They sit glumly at their desks.

Irwin Would you like to start?

Hector I don't mind.

Irwin How do you normally start? It is your lesson. General Studies.

Hector The boys decide. Ask them.

Irwin Anybody?

The boys don't respond.

Hector Come along, boys. Don't sulk.

Dakin We don't know who we are, sir. Your class or Mr Irwin's.

Irwin Does it matter?

Timms Oh yes, sir. It depends if you want us thoughtful. Or smart.

Hector He wants you civil, you rancid little turd. (*Hits him.*)

Timms Look, sir. You're a witness. Hitting us, sir. He could be sacked.

Irwin Settle down. Settle down.
    I thought we might talk about the Holocaust.

Hector Good gracious. Is that on the syllabus?

Irwin It has to be. The syllabus includes the Second War.

Hector I suppose it does.

Irwin Though in any case the scholarship questions aren't limited to a particular curriculum.

70

Hector But how can you teach the Holocaust?

Irwin Well, that would do as a question. Can you . . . should you . . . teach the Holocaust? Anybody?

Akthar It has origins.
It has consequences.
It's a subject like any other.

Scripps Not like any other, surely. Not like any other at all.

Akthar No, but it's a topic.

Hector They go on school trips nowadays, don't they? Auschwitz. Dachau. What has always concerned me is where do they eat their sandwiches? Drink their coke?

Crowther The visitors' centre. It's like anywhere else.

Hector Do they take pictures of each other there? Are they smiling? Do they hold hands? Nothing is appropriate. Just as questions on an examination paper are inappropriate.
How can the boys scribble down an answer however well put that doesn't demean the suffering involved?
And putting it well demeans it as much as putting it badly.

Irwin It's a question of tone, surely. Tact.

Hector Not tact. Decorum.

Lockwood What if you were to write that this was so far beyond one's experience silence is the only proper response.

Dakin That would be your answer to lots of questions, though, wouldn't it, sir?

Hector Yes. Yes, Dakin, it would.

Dakin 'Whereof one cannot speak thereof one must be silent.'

Hector groans and puts his head in his hands.

That's right, isn't it, sir? Wittgenstein.

Irwin Yes. That's good.

Hector No, it's not good. It's . . . flip. It's . . . glib. It's *journalism*.

Dakin But it's you that taught us it.

Hector I didn't teach you and Wittgenstein didn't screw it out of his very guts in order for you to turn it into a dinky formula. I thought that you of all people were bright enough to see that.

Dakin I do see it, sir. Only I don't agree with it. Not . . . not any more.

Timms Sir.

Hector (*head in his hands*) Yes?

Timms You told us once . . . it was to do with the trenches, sir . . . that one person's death tells you more than a thousand. When people are dying like flies, you said, that is what they are dying like.

Posner Except that these weren't just dying. They were being processed. What is different is the process.

Irwin Good.

Hector No, not good.
  Posner is not making a *point*.
  He is speaking from the heart.

Dakin So? Supposing we get a question on Hitler and the Second War and we take your line, sir, that this is not a crazed lunatic but a statesman.

Hector A statesman?

Irwin Not a statesman, Dakin, a politician. I wouldn't say statesman.

72

Dakin Politician, then, and one erratically perhaps, but still discernibly operating within the framework of traditional German foreign policy . . .

Irwin Yes?

Dakin . . . and we go on to say, in accordance with this line, that the death camps have to be seen in the context of this policy.

Pause.

Irwin I think that would be . . . inexpedient.

Hector Inexpedient? Inexpedient?

Irwin I don't think it's true, for a start . . .

Scripps But what has truth got to do with it? I thought that we'd already decided that for the purposes of this examination truth is, if not an irrelevance, then so relative as just to amount to another point of view.

Hector Why can you not simply condemn the camps outright as an unprecedented horror?

There is slight embarrassment.

Lockwood No point, sir. Everybody will do that.
That's the stock answer, sir . . . the camps an event unlike any other, the evil unprecedented, etc., etc.

Hector No. Can't you see that even to say etcetera is monstrous? Etcetera is what the Nazis would have said, the dead reduced to a mere verbal abbreviation.
What have we learned about language?
Orwell. Orwell.

Lockwood All right, not etcetera. But given that the death camps are generally thought of as unique, wouldn't another approach be to show what precedents there were and put them . . . well . . . in proportion?

Scripps Proportion!

Dakin Not proportion then, but putting them in context.

Posner But to put something in context is a step towards saying it can be understood and that it can be explained. And if it can be explained that it can be explained away.

Rudge 'Tout comprendre c'est tout pardonner.'

Hector groans.

Irwin That's good, Posner.

Posner It isn't 'good'. I mean it, sir.

Dakin But when we talk about putting them in context it's only the same as the Dissolution of the Monasteries. After all, monasteries had been dissolved before Henry VIII, dozens of them.

Posner Yes, but the difference is, I didn't lose any relatives in the Dissolution of the Monasteries.

Irwin Good point.

Scripps You keep saying, 'Good point.' Not good point, sir. True. To you the Holocaust is just another topic on which we may get a question.

Irwin No. But this is history. Distance yourselves.

Our perspective on the past alters. Looking back, immediately in front of us is dead ground. We don't see it and because we don't see it this means that there is no period so remote as the recent past and one of the historian's jobs is to anticipate what our perspective of that period will be . . . even on the Holocaust.

The bell goes.

Irwin I thought that went rather well.

Hector Parrots. I thought I was lining their minds with some sort of literary insulation, proof against the primacy of fact. Instead back come my words like a Speak Your Weight Machine. 'Tout comprendre c'est tout pardonner.' Ugh.

Irwin I was rather encouraged. They're getting the idea.

Hector Do you know what the worst thing is? I wanted them to show off, to come up with the short answer, the handy quote. I wanted them to compete.
It's time I went.

Irwin Went where?

Dakin and Scripps come in, a touch awkardly.

Hector Oh, home. Home.
Oh, Dakin, I've got the *Statesman* for you in the staff room.

Dakin I'll get it tomorrow, sir.
I just want to ask Mr Irwin something.

He waits until Hector goes.

We were having a discussion, sir, as to whether you are disingenuous or meretricious.

Irwin I'm flattered.

Dakin Disingenuous is insincere, not candid, having secret motives.
Meretricious is showy and falsely attractive.
We decided, sir, you were meretricious but not disingenuous.

Irwin Thank you.

Dakin What you were saying about the perspective altering, sir . . .

The stuff we generally do with Mr Hector, the poetry, Shakespeare and all that, will the perspective alter on that?

Irwin Not now, no, probably not.

Scripps Better shelf-life than your stuff, then, sir.

Irwin That's the point. It's art. It has a different shelf-life altogether.

Dakin Never mind, coach. (*He pats him on the back.*) We still love you, even if you are a bit flash.

Irwin goes.

Scripps You flirt.

Dakin I don't understand it. I have never wanted to please anybody the way I do him, girls not excepted.

Scripps It's this making it up I can't get used to. Arguing for effect. Not believing what you're saying. That's not history. It's journalism.

Dakin Just wait till you get started on sex. You're making it up all the time. Being different, outrageous. That's what they go for. I tell you, history is fucking.

Scripps Discuss.

Anyway I'm not going to, am I? Not while God's still in the frame?

Dakin Hector's gone right off me.

Scripps Lucky you.

Dakin Thinks I've gone over to the enemy.

Scripps I did notice the lifts seem to have stopped.

Dakin No. That's something else.
He's going, you know.

Scripps The big man?

Dakin Don't let on. Fiona says.

Scripps Sacked? Who complained?

Dakin shrugs.

That's why the lifts have stopped.

Dakin Poor sod. Though in some ways I'm not sorry.

Scripps No. No more genital massage as one speeds along leafy suburban roads.
No more the bike's melancholy long withdrawing roar as he dropped you at the corner, your honour still intact.

Dakin Lecher though one is, or aspires to be, it occurs to me that the lot of woman cannot be easy, who must suffer such inexpert male fumblings virtually on a daily basis.
Are we scarred for life, do you think?

Scripps We must hope so.
Perhaps it will turn me into Proust.

Headmaster's study.

Headmaster A letter from the Posner parents. Charming couple. Jewish of course. Father a furrier, retired and, I suspect, elderly. Posner a . . . Benjamin is it . . .? A child of their old age.

Irwin He's clever.

Headmaster Jewish boys often are, a role though nowadays that is more and more being taken over by the

Asian boys, intelligence to some degree the fruit of discrimination.

It was apropos the Holocaust.

Irwin It came up in discussion.

Headmaster As it should. A shaping circumstance. A line drawn. Before and after.

However, Posner *père*, who seems a little overexcited, has taken some exception to your remarks that it should be kept in proportion.

Irwin I didn't quite say that.

Headmaster Mr Posner calls it 'a unique historical event' and says that it can't be compared with the Dissolution of the Monasteries.

Well, who in his right mind would think it could?

Irwin We did discuss how the Holocaust should be tackled in the event of them getting a question on it.

Headmaster Prefaced presumably with all the right disclaimers?

No suggestion above all that it didn't happen.

Irwin No, no . . . only the boys were asking.

Headmaster (*suddenly angry*) I'm not concerned with what the boys were asking. What concerns me is what you were telling them.

Irwin I was telling them that there were ways of discussing it that went beyond mere lamentation. The risk the historian . . .

Headmaster Mr Irwin. Fuck the historian.

I have two angry Jewish parents threatening to complain to the school governors. I have explained to them that you are young and inexperienced and that your anxiety that the boys should do well has perhaps outrun your sense of proportion.

You will write them a letter of apology on much the same lines.

They also complain that Hector has had the boy singing hymns.

Irwin Posner likes singing.

Headmaster Hymns?

Irwin Anything.

Headmaster Not . . . Gracie Fields?

Irwin Possibly.

Headmaster Didn't I suggest you grew a moustache?

Posner sings a verse of Gracie Fields' 'Sing as We Go'.

Irwin Do you tell them everything that goes on at school?

Posner He's old, my father. He's interested. I just said the Holocaust was a historical fact like other historical facts.
  It was my uncle who hit me.

Irwin I'm sorry. It was my fault. I was too . . . dispassionate, I suppose. The Holocaust is not yet an abstract question. Though in time, of course, it will be.

Pause.

No more singing, too, I gather?

Posner Not hymns. They're fine with Barbra Streisand.

Pause.

Sir, sorry to keep on about it, but if the Holocaust does come up . . .

Irwin At home?

Posner No, as a question.

Irwin Surprise them. You're Jewish. You can get away with a lot more than the other candidates.

Equivalent would be Akthar singing the praises of empire.

But . . . say what you think.

Posner They don't send your papers home?

Dakin My duty to Your Lordship.

Irwin (*going*) Your essays, so called, are on the table.

Dakin I really enjoyed doing this one. And I'm beginning to get it. Turning facts on their head. It's like a game. (*He looks at his mark.*) Shit. He never gives an inch, does he? 'Lucid and up to a point compelling but if you reach a conclusion it escaped me.'

Scripps Have you looked at your handwriting recently?

Dakin Why?

Scripps You're beginning to write like him.

Dakin I'm not trying to, honestly.

Scripps You're writing like him, too.

Posner No, I'm not. Dakin writes like him. I write like Dakin.

Dakin It's done wonders for the sex life.

Apparently I talk about him so much Fiona gets really pissed off. Doing it is about the only time I shut up.

Scripps Would you do it with him?

Dakin I wondered about that. I might. Bring a little sunshine into his life. It's only a wank, after all.

Scripps What makes you think he'd do it with you?

Dakin smiles.

You complacent fuck.

Dakin Does the Archbishop of Canterbury know you talk like this?

Scripps So you broke through with Fiona. The Western Front.

Dakin Broke through. Had the Armistice. The Treaty of Versailles. It's now the Weimar Republic.

Scripps Decadence?

Dakin nods happily.

Posner Aren't you frightened it's all going to be over too soon?

Dakin What, sex?

Posner I mean, what have you got to look forward to?

Dakin More of the same. You can't save it up. I like him. I just wish I thought he liked me. (*He goes.*)

Posner Irwin does like him.
He seldom looks at anyone else.

Scripps How do you know?

Posner Because nor do I. Our eyes meet, looking at Dakin.

Scripps Oh Poz, with your spaniel heart, it will pass.

Posner Yes, it's only a phase.
Who says I want it to pass?
But the pain. The pain.

Scripps Hector would say it's the only education worth having.

Posner I just wish there were marks for it.

*Hector, Irwin and Mrs Lintott are sitting behind the
table, pretending to be the examination board.*

Irwin Anything provocative in your papers and they may
question you on that. Otherwise they are likely to be the
usual, 'What are your hobbies?' type questions.

Mrs Lintott Mr Akthar. You say you're interested in
architecture. Who is your favourite architect?

Akthar Richard Rogers.

Mrs Lintott I was thinking more along Wren–Hawksmoor
lines. Richard Rogers? Doesn't he write musicals?

Akthar Oh, miss. It's a different one. You wouldn't get
far, miss.

Mrs Lintott Nor will you. Next. Now, Mr Crowther.
One of your interests is the theatre. Tell us about that.

Crowther I'm keen on acting. I've done various parts,
favourite being . . .

Irwin Can I stop you?
  Don't mention the theatre.

Crowther It's what I'm interested in.

Irwin Then soft pedal it, the acting side of it anyway.
  Dons . . . most dons anyway . . . think the theatre is a
waste of time. In their view any undergraduate keen on
acting forfeits all hope of a good degree.

Hector So much for Shakespeare.

Irwin It's not the plays, it's the acting of the plays,
Shakespeare, anybody. It's no fun teaching the stage-struck.

Hector And isn't being stage-struck part of their
education?

82

Posner Music is all right though, isn't it, sir? They don't frown on that.

Hector No. You should just say what you enjoy.

Posner Mozart.

Irwin No, no. everyone likes Mozart.
Somebody more off the beaten track. Tippett, say, or Bruckner.

Posner But I don't know them.

Hector May I make a suggestion? Why can they not all just tell the truth?

Irwin It's worth trying, provided, of course, you can make it seem like you're telling the truth.

Hector Oh, yes, a degree of presentation.
Dorothy. Have you anything you'd like to add?

Mrs Lintott I hesitate to mention this, lest it occasion a sophisticated groan, but it may not have crossed your minds that one of the dons who interviews you may be a woman.
I'm reluctant at this stage in the game to expose you to new ideas, but having taught you all history on a strictly non-gender-orientated basis I just wonder whether it occurs to any of you how dispiriting this can be?
It's obviously dispiriting to you, Dakin, or you wouldn't be yawning.

Dakin Sorry, miss.

Mrs Lintott Women so seldom get a turn for a start, Elizabeth I less remarkable for her abilities than that, unlike most of her sisters, she did get a chance to exercise them.
Am I embarrassing you?

Timms A bit, miss.

Mrs Lintott Why?

Timms It's not our fault, miss. It's just the way it is.

Lockwood 'The world is everything that is the case,' miss. Wittgenstein, miss.

Mrs Lintott I know it's Wittgenstein, thank you. Tell me, just out of interest, did he travel on the other bus?

Hector Bus? Bus? What bus?

Irwin On the few occasions he went anywhere, yes, I believe he did.

Mrs Lintott You can tell.
   Because 'The world is everything that is the case' seems actually rather a feminine approach to things: rueful, accepting, taking things as you find them.
   A real man would be trickier: 'The world is everything that can be made to seem the case.'
   However, je divague.
   Can you, for a moment, imagine how dispiriting it is to teach five centuries of masculine ineptitude?
   Why do you think there are no women historians on TV?

Timms No tits?

Hector Hit that boy. Hit him.

Timms Sir! You can't, sir.

Hector I'm not hitting you. He is. And besides, you're not supposed to say tits. Hit him again!

Mrs Lintott I'll tell you why there are no women historians on TV, it's because they don't get carried away for a start, and they don't come bouncing up to you with every new historical notion they've come up with . . . the bow-wow school of history.
   History's not such a frolic for women as it is for men. Why should it be? They never get round the conference

84

table. In 1919, for instance, they just arranged the flowers then gracefully retired.

History is a commentary on the various and continuing incapabilities of men.

What is history? History is women following behind with the bucket.

And I'm not asking you to espouse this point of view but the occasional nod in its direction can do you no harm.

There is a silence.

Mrs Lintott You should note, boys, that your masters find this undisguised expression of feeling distasteful, as, I see, do some of you.

Irwin Rudge?

Rudge is interviewed.

Mrs Lintott Now. How do you define history, Mr Rudge?

Rudge Can I speak freely, miss? Without being hit.

Mrs Lintott I will protect you.

Rudge How do I define history?
It's just one fucking thing after another.

Hector makes a moves to hit him but is forestalled.

Mrs Lintott I see. And why do you want to come to Christ Church?

Rudge It's the one I thought I might get into.

Irwin No other reason?

Rudge shakes his head.

Mrs Lintott Do you like the architecture, for instance?

Rudge They'll ask me about sport, won't they?

Mrs Lintott If you're as uncommunicative as this they may be forced to.

Hector The point is, Rudge, that even if they want to take you on the basis of your prowess on the field you have to help them to pretend at least that there are other considerations.

Rudge thinks.

Rudge I'm keen on a film.

Irwin What film?

Rudge Well, lots of films, only Miss said to say film not films.

Mrs Lintott No, Rudge. What I said was that it sounds better to say 'I'm keen on film' rather than 'I like films'.

Irwin Like what?

Rudge thinks.

Lockwood Say, *This Sporting Life*.

Rudge shakes his head.

It's about rugger.

Rudge I'd like to see that. Is it recent?

Look, I'm shit at all this. Sorry.

If they like me and they want to take me they'll take me because I'm dull and ordinary. I'm no good in interviews but I've got enough chat to take me round the golf course and maybe there'll be someone on the board who wants to go round the golf course.

You think that's a joke, but golf makes the same sense to me as architecture or films do to you. You may not rate it but it's an accomplishment. I may not know much about Jean-Paul Sartre, but I've got a handicap of four.

Mrs Lintott Where have you heard about Sartre?

Rudge He was a good golfer.

Hector Really. I never knew that. Interesting.

Bell goes.

Irwin Remember also, our puny efforts notwithstanding, you will be up against boys and girls who will have been taught better than you.

Hector Taught differently, anyway.

Hector and Mrs Lintott go.

Lockwood How did you know Sartre was a golfer?

Rudge I don't know that he was. How could I? I don't even know who the fuck he is. Well, they keep telling us you have to lie.

Crowther I've a feeling Kafka was good at table tennis.

Akthar Yes?

Crowther I'll be glad when we can be shot of all this shit.

Dakin is left with Irwin.

Dakin Sir, I never gave you my essay.

Irwin That's good.

Dakin What degree did you get, sir?
You've never said.

Irwin A second.

Dakin Boring. Didn't the old magic work?

Irwin I hadn't perfected the technique.

Dakin What college were you at?

Irwin Corpus.

Dakin That's not one anybody is going in for.

Irwin No.

Dakin You happy?

Irwin There? Yes. Yes, I was, quite.

This is quite a pausy conversation, with Dakin more master than pupil.

Dakin Do you think we'll be happy . . . say we get in?

Irwin You'll be happy anyway.

Dakin I'm not sure I like that. Why?

Irwin shrugs.

Uncomplicated, is that what you mean?
Outgoing?
Straight?

Irwin None of them bad things to be.

Dakin Depends. Nice to be a bit more complicated.

Irwin Or to be thought so.
How's Posner?

Dakin Why?

Irwin He likes you, doesn't he?

Dakin It's his age.
He's growing up.

Irwin Hard for him.

Dakin Boring for me.
You're not suggesting I do something about it. It happens.
I wouldn't anyway.
Too young.

Irwin says nothing.

You still look quite young.

Irwin That's because I am, I suppose.

There is an interminable pause.

Dakin How do you think history happens?

Irwin What?

Dakin How does stuff happen, do you think?
People decide to do stuff.
Make moves. Alter things.

Irwin I'm not sure what you're talking about.

Dakin No? (*He smiles.*) Think about it.

Irwin Some do . . . make moves, I suppose.
Others react to events.
In 1939 Hitler made a move on Poland.
Poland . . .

Dakin . . . gave in.

Irwin (*simultaneously*) . . . defended itself.

Irwin Is that what you mean?

Dakin (*unperturbed*) No.
Not Poland anyway.
Was Poland taken by surprise?

Irwin To some extent.
Though they knew something was up.
What was your essay about?

Dakin Turning points.

Irwin Oh yes. Moments when history rattles over the
points.
Shall I tell you what you've written?
Dunkirk?

Dakin Yes.

Irwin Hitler turning on Russia?

Dakin Yes.

Irwin Alamein?

Dakin Yes.

Irwin More? Oh, that's good.

Dakin Two actually.

The first one: when Chamberlain resigned as Prime Minister in 1940 Churchill wasn't the first thought; Halifax more generally acceptable.

But on the afternoon when the decision was taken Halifax chose to go to the dentist. If Halifax had had better teeth we might have lost the war.

Irwin Very good. Terrific.

And the other one?

Dakin Well, it is Alamein, but not the battle. Montgomery took over the Eighth Army before Alamein but he wasn't the first choice. Churchill had appointed General Gott. Gott was flying home to London in an unescorted plane when, purely by chance, a lost German fighter spotted his plane and shot him down. So it was Montgomery who took over, seeing this afterwards, of course, as the hand of God.

Irwin That's brilliant. First class.

Dakin It's a good game.

Irwin It's more than a game. Thinking about what might have happened alerts you to the consequences of what did.

Dakin It's subjunctive history.

Irwin Come again.

Dakin The subjunctive is the mood you use when something might or might not have happened, when it's imagined.

90

Hector is crazy about the subjunctive.
Why are you smiling?

Irwin Nothing. Good luck.

Boys and staff all come on as the boys arrange the chairs for a photograph.

Posner All my life I've been one of those squatting at the front. I don't care about Oxford and Cambridge. I'd just like to graduate to a chair.

Mrs Lintott moves up.

Mrs Lintott Posner, sit here. Rudge, you go down there.

She moves up and he sits on the front row.

Akthar Ready.

They are all ready for the picture when the Headmaster turns up.

Headmaster A photograph? Always a good idea.
Dorothy, sit here. Then I can go here. Posner, you'll be better on the floor.
Who's taking the picture?

Akthar It's delayed action.

Headmaster No, no. Too much hit-and-miss.
Hector, why don't you take it?

Mrs Lintott Then he won't be in the picture.

Headmaster Hector doesn't mind.

Mrs Lintott The boys might.

Headmaster It isn't for the boys. It's for the school.
Rudge, floor, Akthar.

91

Now, boys. Look like Oxbridge material.
No negative thoughts. Threshold of great things.

Hector 'Magnificently unprepared
For the long littleness of life.'

*The boys do a farewell song and dance of Gracie Fields'
'Wish Me Luck as You Wave Me Goodbye', then go off,
leaving Irwin and Mrs Lintott waiting to see the
Headmaster. Very flat and empty.*

Irwin What's he want us for?

Mrs Lintott No idea.

Irwin Pep talk?

Mrs Lintott Bit late for that, it's probably about Hector.

Irwin I sort of know.

Mrs Lintott I imagine everyone sort of knows.

Irwin Does his wife?

Mrs Lintott He doesn't think so, apparently, but I imagine
she's another one who's sort of known all along. A husband
on a low light, that's what they want, these supposedly
unsuspecting wives, the man's lukewarm attentions just
what they married them for.

He's a fool. He was also unlucky.

For a start Mrs Headmaster didn't normally do a stint
at Age Concern on a Wednesday unless someone was off.
And what if a customer had come in just as Hector had
got to the lights and she'd been looking the other way?
Or the lights had been green? This smallest of incidents,
the junction of a dizzying range of alternatives any one of
which could have had a different outcome. If I was a bold

teacher . . . if I was you, even . . . I could spend a lesson
dissecting what the Headmaster insists on calling 'this
unfortunate incident' and it would teach the boys more
about history and the utter randomness of things than . . .
well, than I've ever managed to do so far.

Irwin I wonder how they're going on.

Mrs Lintott Don't you ever want to go back?

Irwin To Oxford? Not clever enough.
Not . . . anything enough really.

Pause.

I used to imagine myself doing research and coming up
with something startling, a new way of looking at things.
Like Namier, say.
And I would do it, then fling it in their faces.

Mrs Lintott Oxford? Why should they care? No. They're
like everybody else. Make money, that's what they
admire. Make lots of money then don't give them any.

Headmaster comes out with Hector.

Headmaster Dorothy, a word?

They go back into the study.

Hector Trouble at t' mill.
That's the news he's aching to impart.
My . . . marching orders.

Irwin I sort of knew.

Hector Ah.

Irwin Dakin told me.

Hector Did he tell you why?

Irwin nods.

I've got this idea of buying a van, filling it with books and taking it round country markets . . . Shropshire, Herefordshire. 'The open road, the dusty highway. Travel, change, interest, excitement. Poop, poop.'

Pause.

I didn't want to turn out boys who in later life had a deep love of literature, or who would talk in middle age of the lure of language and their love of words. Words said in that reverential way that is somehow Welsh. That's what the tosh is for. *Brief Encounter*, Gracie Fields, it's an antidote. Sheer calculated silliness.

Irwin Has a boy ever made you unhappy?

Hector They used to do.

See it as an inoculation, rather. Briefly painful but providing immunity for however long it takes. With the occasional booster . . . another face, a reminder of the pain . . . it can last you half a lifetime.

Irwin Love.

Hector Who could love me? I talk too much.

Irwin It took me by surprise.

Hector Don't do it.

Irwin I wouldn't dare.

Hector No. Don't teach.

Irwin I wasn't intending to.

Hector Who intends to?

Six months, a year. Till something more exciting turns up. It's always the same. I used to think I could warm myself on the vitality of the boys I taught, but that doesn't work.

It ought to renew . . . the young mind; warm, eager, trusting; instead comes . . . a kind of coarsening. You

94

start to clown. Plus a fatigue that passes for philosophy but is nearer to indifference.

Now boys come and go but I am no more moved by this than by the arrival and departure of trains.

Boys have become work.

Irwin Do they know?

Hector They know everything.
Don't touch him. He'll think you're a fool.
That's what they think about me.
I'm lucky, I suppose. Dodging the ignominy.
Still, I'd have liked to have served my time.

Mrs Lintott comes out of the study.

I gather you knew, too.

Mrs Lintott smiles.

And the boys knew.

Mrs Lintott Well, of course the boys knew. They had it at first hand.

Hector I didn't actually do anything. It was a laying-on of hands, I don't deny that, but more in benediction than gratification or anything else.

Mrs Lintott Hector, darling, love you as I do, that is the most colossal balls.

Hector Is it?

Mrs Lintott A grope is a grope. It is not the Annunciation.
You . . . twerp.
Anyway what Felix wanted to tell me is that when I finish next year he's hoping he can persuade you to step into my shoes.

The Headmaster comes out.

Headmaster Irwin –

Mrs Lintott For your information they're a size seven court shoe, broad fitting.

Irwin goes into the study.

Scripps I attended Eucharist in the college chapel where, apart from a girl from a school in West Bromwich, I was the only communicant. It was a genuine act of worship, though I knew it would do me no harm with the college, the self-servingness of my devotions in this instance leaving me untroubled. I really wanted to get in. I have never particularly liked myself but the boy I was, kneeling in that cold and empty chapel that winter morning, fills me now with longing and pity.

Dakin The guy whose room I had seemed a bit of a pillock. There was a *Lord of the Rings* poster for a start and an Arsenal scarf draped round a photograph of Virginia Woolf, only I think maybe this was irony. No books much, except he had a book with lists of everybody who'd been at other colleges, so I looked at that for a bit. Oh, and I went and looked at Corpus where Irwin was.

No sex.

Posner I sat in the room most of the time or trailed around the streets. I can see why they make a fuss about it. Every college is like a stately home; my parents would love it. There was a question on the Holocaust. And I did play it down.

They asked me about it at the interview. Praised what they called my sense of detachment.

Said it was the foundation of writing history.

I think I did well.

96

The boys erupt onto the stage.

Headmaster Splendid news! Posner a scholarship, Dakin an exhibition and places for everyone else. It's more than one could ever have hoped for. Irwin, you are to be congratulated, a remarkable achievement. And you too, Dorothy, of course, who laid the foundations.

Mrs Lintott Not Rudge, Headmaster.

Headmaster Not Rudge? Oh dear.

Irwin He has said nothing. The others have all had letters.

Headmaster It was always an outside chance. I felt we were indulging him by allowing him to enter at all. That college must think we're fools. A pity. It would have been good to have a clean sweep.
   Ah, Rudge.
   You . . . you haven't heard from Oxford?

Rudge No, sir.

Mrs Lintott Perhaps you'll hear tomorrow.

Rudge Why should I? They told me when I was there.

Irwin I'm sorry.

Rudge What for? I got in.

Irwin How come?

Rudge How come they told me or how come they took a thick sod like me?
   I had family connections.

Headmaster Somebody in your family went to Christ Church?

Rudge In a manner of speaking.
   My dad. Before he got married he was a college servant there. This old parson guy was just sitting there for most

97

of the interview, suddenly said was I related to Bill Rudge who'd been a scout on Staircase 7 in the 1950s. So I said he was my dad and they said I was just the kind of candidate they were looking for, college servant's son, now an undergraduate, evidence of how far they had come, wheel come full circle and that.

Mind you, I did all the other stuff like Stalin was a sweetie and Wilfred Owen was a wuss. They said I was plainly someone who thought for himself and just what the college rugger team needed.

Dakin In the room I stayed in there was a handbook to the colleges, list of previous undergraduates and that.

I looked you up only you weren't there.

Irwin I'm surprised you were interested.

Dakin I was kind of lonely. I thought it would be nice to see your name.

Irwin You maybe looked at the wrong list.

Dakin Corpus?

Irwin No, I said I was at Jesus.

Dakin You said you were at Corpus.

Irwin No.

Dakin You did.

Irwin Corpus, Jesus. What does it matter?

Dakin Because I went round to look at the fucking college, that's why it matters.

Because I imagined you there.

Pause.

Irwin I never got in.

I was at Bristol.

I did go to Oxford, but it was just to do a teaching diploma.

Does that make a difference?

Dakin To what? To me? (*He shrugs.*)

At least you lied. And lying's good, isn't it? We've established that.

Lying works.

Except you ought to learn to do it properly.

Pause.

Anybody else, I'd say we could have a drink.

Irwin Yes?

I can't tonight.

Dakin Tomorrow then?

Irwin That's bad, too.

Dakin Is that a euphemism? It is, isn't it?

Have a drink.

Saying 'a drink' when you mean something else.

Only a euphemism is a nice way of saying something nasty. Whereas a drink is a nice way of saying something nice.

Irwin I think that's a euphemism, too.

Dakin Actually, forget the euphemism.

I'm just kicking the tyres on this one but, further to the drink, what I was really wondering was whether there were any circumstances in which there was any chance of your sucking me off.

Pause.

Or something similar.

Pause.

Actually that would please Hector.

Irwin What?

Dakin 'Your sucking me off.'
It's a gerund. He likes gerunds.
And your being scared shitless, that's another gerund.

Irwin I didn't know you were that way inclined.

Dakin I'm not, but it's the end of term; I've got into Oxford; I thought we might push the boat out.

Pause.

Anyway, I'll leave it on the table. (*He is ready to go but turns back.*) I don't understand this.
  Reckless; impulsive; immoral . . . how come there's such a difference between the way you teach and the way you live?

Irwin Actually, it's amoral.

Dakin Is it fuck. 'No need to tell the truth.' That's immoral.

Irwin I could dispute that with you.

Dakin Over a drink? Or whatever? No.
  Why are you so bold in argument and talking but when it comes to the point, when it's something that's actually happening, I mean now, you're so fucking careful?
  Is it because you're a teacher and I'm . . . a boy?

Irwin Obviously that . . .

Dakin Why? Who cares? I don't.

Irwin You've already had to cope with one master who touches you up. I don't . . .

Dakin Is that what it is?
Is it that you don't want to be like Hector?
You won't be.
You can't be.
How can you be?
Hector's a joke.

Irwin No he isn't. He isn't.

Dakin That side of him is.

Irwin This . . . it's . . . it's such a cliché.

Dakin Right. And you abhor clichés, don't you?
And you teach us to avoid them. Nothing worse.
Nothing more likely to put the examiners off.
But in this subject there are no examiners.
And I'll tell you something. Clichés can be quite fun.
That's how they got to be clichés.
So give yourself a break. Be like everybody else for a change. On this one you don't have to be different.

Irwin All right.

Dakin All right what?

Irwin All right, let's have a drink. (*He takes out his diary.*)

Dakin No. Don't take out your sodding diary.
Keep it in your head.
Or here. (*He points to his heart*).

Irwin Maybe next week.

Dakin Get this man. Next week? You can suck me off next week. I've heard of a crowded schedule but this is ridiculous. I bet you have a purse, don't you?

Irwin Yes, I do, actually.

Dakin God, we've got a long way to go.
Do you ever take your glasses off?

Irwin Why?

Dakin It's a start.

Irwin Not with me. Taking off my glasses is the last thing I do.

Dakin Yes? I'll look forward to it.
What do you do on a Sunday afternoon?
What are you doing this Sunday afternoon?

Irwin I was going to be working, going through the accounts of Roche Abbey. It was a Cistercian house just to the south of Doncaster. Only I think I just had a better offer.

Dakin I think you did. And we're not in the subjunctive either. It is going to happen.

Dakin I just wanted to say thank you.

Scripps So? Give him a subscription to *The Spectator* or a box of Black Magic. Just because you've got a scholarship doesn't mean you've got to give him unfettered access to your dick.

Dakin So how would you say thank you?

Scripps Same as you, probably. On my knees.

Dakin Also – this is the big triumph – I had a session with Felix. I asked him what the difference was between Hector touching us up on the bike and him trying to feel up Fiona.

Scripps You are insane.

Dakin He was upset naturally, and the language was shocking, but eventually he took the point, and the upshot is, Hector is reprieved. He stays.

Scripps So everybody's happy.

Dakin I hadn't realised how easy it is to make things happen. You know?

Scripps No.
    Actually I shouldn't have said everybody's happy, as just saying the words meant, like in a play, that the laws of irony were thereby activated and things began to unravel pretty quickly after that.

Dakin Now look, everybody. This is known as Posner's reward.

He hugs Posner.

Posner Is that it?
    The longed-for moment?

Dakin What's wrong with it?

Posner Too fucking brief. I was looking for something more . . . lingering.

The boys hoot for more so Dakin does it again.

Posner And is that Hector's reward?

Dakin I thought I would. *(putting on the motorcycle helmet)* It's only polite. Just for old times' sake.

Scripps Just don't let him go past the charity shop.

Hector comes in, clad in his leathers and cheerful now that he has been reprieved.

Rudge Sir. Is the jackpot still going?

Hector Why?

Rudge I've got something.

Hector Just you?

Rudge Yes.

Hector I'm listening.

*Rudge sings a verse of a song (The Pet Shop Boys'
'It's a Sin').*

Rudge (*sings*)
'At school they taught me how to be
So pure in thought and word and deed
They didn't quite suceed
For everything I long to do
No matter when or where or who
Has one thing in common too
It's a, it's a, it's a, it's a sin
It's a sin.'

Timms He doesn't know that.
You can't expect him to know that.

Rudge I do.

Timms And anyway it's crap.

Rudge So is Gracie Fields. Only that's his crap. This is
our crap.

Hector Excuse me, children. Easy though I am to
overlook, I am here. Unsurprisingly, I do not know the
song in question.

Akthar Pop is the new literacy, sir. I read it.

Hector In which case, I am now illiterate. But Rudge is
right . . . his crap or my crap, it makes no difference. So,
in another reference to our ancient popular culture, I say,
'Give him the money, Barney!'

Headmaster comes in.

Headmaster What is this?
A boy in a motorcycle helmet?
Who is it? Dakin?
No, no, no.

Under no circumstances.
Hector, I thought I'd made this plain.

Hector (whose fault it isn't, after all) just shrugs.

Take somebody else . . . take . . .

Scripps And here history rattled over the points . . .

Irwin has come in.

Headmaster Take Irwin.

Hector Irwin?

Irwin Sure, why not?

Dakin gives him the helmet.

Dakin Hang on to your briefcase.

Irwin Fuck.
Off. Fuck right off.

Scripps There are various theories about what happened,
why he came off. It's inconceivable he ever touched Irwin,
who would in any case have been clutching his briefcase.
Or it may be Hector was so used to driving with one
hand while the other was busy behind him that driving
with two made him put on speed.

These explanations are a touch obvious which, if he
taught us anything, Irwin taught us not to be. So I think
that, since Irwin had never been on the back of a bike
before, going round the corner he leaned out instead of in
and so unbalanced Hector. That would be appropriate,
too. Trust Irwin to lean the opposite way to everyone else.

Irwin (*now in a wheelchair*) With no memory of what
happened I am of no help. I only know what I have been
told, my last memory Dakin asking me for a drink.

Something we never did, incidentally.

Dakin No. It was the wheelchair. That's terrible, isn't it?
   Afterwards I couldn't face the wheelchair. Still. At least
I asked him. And barring accidents it would have
happened.

Rudge There is no barring accidents. It's what I said.
History is just one fucking thing after another.

Scripps Someone dies at school and you remember it all
your life.

*The staff, Irwin in his wheelchair and the boys, who sing
a verse of 'Bye Bye, Blackbird', during which we see on
the video screen photographs of Hector as a young man.*

Headmaster If I speak of Hector it is of enthusiasm
shared, passion conveyed and seeds sown of future
harvest. He loved language. He loved words. For each
and every one of you, his pupils, he opened a deposit
account in the bank of literature and made you all
shareholders in that wonderful world of words.

Timms Some of the things he said . . . or quoted anyway,
you never knew when it was which:
   'We are mulched by the dead, though one person's
death will tell you more than a thousand.'

Lockwood There was the time he put his head down on
the desk and said, 'What am I doing teaching in this god-
forsaken school?' It was the first time I realised a teacher
was a human being.

Akthar There was a contract between him and his class.
Quite what the contract was or what it involved would
be hard to say. But it was there.

Crowther He was stained and shabby and did unforgivable things but he led you to expect the best.

Even his death was a lesson and added to the store.

Mrs Lintott Hector never bothered with what he was educating these boys for. They become solicitors, chartered accountants, teachers even, members of what used to be called the professional classes.

Two of these boys become magistrates.

Crowther and Lockwood put up their hands.

One a headmaster.

Akthar puts up hand.

Pillars of a community that no longer has much use for pillars.

One puts together a chain of dry-cleaners and takes drugs at the weekend.

Timms puts up hand.

Another is a tax lawyer, telling highly paid fibs and making frequent trips to the Gulf States.

Dakin acknowledges.

Dakin I like money. It's fun.

Mrs Lintott One is a builder who carpets the Dales in handy homes.

Rudge does not put his hand up.

Rudge Is that meant to be me? I'm not putting my hand up to that. Like them or not, Rudge Homes are at least affordable homes for first-time buyers.

Mrs Lintott All right, Rudge.

Rudge Death, it's just one more excuse to patronise. I had years of that.

Mrs Lintott Same here.

If I may proceed?

Hector had seen Irwin turning his boys into journalists but in the event there is only one . . . and on a better class of paper, a career he is always threatening to abandon in order, as he puts it, 'really to write'.

Scripps puts up his hand.

Irwin Hector said *I* was a journalist.

Mrs Lintott And so you were. Briefly at the school and then on TV. I enjoyed your programmes but they were more journalism than history. What you call yourself now you're in politics I'm not sure.

Irwin I'm not in politics. Who's in politics? I'm in government.

Mrs Lintott Well you're not in monastic history, that's for sure. Hector would have been surprised and gratified too, to find himself regularly recalled in the *Old Boys' Letter* few of them can otherwise be bothered to read.

Still, of all Hector's boys, there is only one who truly took everything to heart, remembers everything he was ever taught . . . the songs, the poems, the sayings, the endings; the words of Hector never forgotten.

Posner looks at boys on either side before putting his hand up.

He lives alone in a cottage he has renovated himself, has an allotment and periodic breakdowns.

He haunts the local library and keeps a scrapbook of the achievements of his one-time classmates and has a host of friends . . . though only on the internet, and none in his right name or even gender. He has long since stopped asking himself where it went wrong.

Hector Finish, good lady, the bright day is done and we are for the dark.

Irwin He was a good man but I do not think there is time for his kind of teaching any more.

Scripps No. Love apart, it is the only education worth having.

Hector Pass the parcel.
  That's sometimes all you can do.
  Take it, feel it and pass it on.
  Not for me, not for you, but for someone, somewhere, one day.
  Pass it on, boys.
  That's the game I wanted you to learn.
  Pass it on.

End.